MODEL FOR A HUMANISTIC EDUCATION:
EDUCATION:
THE DANISH
FOLK HIGHSCHOOL

STUDIES OF THE PERSON

edited by

Carl R. Rogers
William R. Coulson

RVTSA

MODEL FOR A HUMANISTIC EDUCATION:
THE DANISH
FOLK HIGHSCHOOL

David C. L. Davis

CHARLES E. MERRILL PUBLISHING COMPANY

A Bell & Howell Company   Columbus, Ohio

International Standard Book Number: 0–675–09190–X

Library of Congress Catalog Card Number: 74–155262

1 2 3 4 5 6 7 8 9 10—75 74 73 72 71

FOREWORD

It is always exciting to discover, as we do in this book, that "new ideas" are also old ones, and that they have been tested in the crucible of experience. In this country today many writers are concerned about the absurd relationship between our outdated educational system and the ever-changing modern world. Students are being "turned off" in droves. Universities—and even high schools—have become the target for futile riots which simply give vent to the explosive frustrations of their students. Teachers and educators who for years have avoided asking for any meaningful feedback from those who have been through the educational process are now receiving, unasked, protests, demonstrations, demands, which would have been more constructive had they been given and received while they were in a cooler and more formative state.

In this very real crisis the giant educational bureaucracies are in many instances stirring and moving—slowly perhaps, but moving. But in what directions shall they move? Books are pouring into the market, written by people with experience as teachers, endeavoring to point out some of the ways in which schools and colleges might become more closely related to life as it is lived; might stimulate curiosity and self-initiated learning, rather than withering these precious and tender plants. I suspect the experience which Dr. Coulson and I have had, as editors of this series, is typical. We have received a surprising number of manuscripts with a thrust toward the renewal and invigoration of the educational system. In addition to a considerable number of manuscripts of this nature which for various reasons we have not accepted, there are now in the series: Hal Lyon's volume on the ways in which feelings can be incorporated into the learning process, thus making it an education of the whole man; [1] Dillon's honest account of his halting, struggling, imperfect attempt to bring

---

[1] Lyon, H. C., Jr. *Learning to Feel—Feeling to Learn.*

spontaneity, and inquiry, and open interpersonal relationships into the rigidity of a high school classroom; [2] Kline's concern with the personal quest in learning; [3] and my own attempt to give support and help, and ideological underpinning to those who would like to become not teachers, but facilitators of learning.[4] There are other such manuscripts on the way to publication. So there are many concerned educators who are working hard to help schools at all levels to discover constructive pathways from which they can choose.

The reaction of many within the educational system to these ideas is that they are too chancy, not sufficiently supported by the evidence. They hesitate to leave behind the practices they have always known, horribly inadequate as they may be, to adopt approaches which they regard as untried.

Here is where this book comes in, with two very convincing aspects. In the first place it is based on the author's personal experience, which gives it a down-to-earth feeling. More importantly, it describes the way in which some of today's "new ideas" in education worked out a century ago in Denmark. Bringing to light the experiment carried on in the little-known Danish Folk High-schools so long ago should strengthen many an innovative educator in this country today. There is just enough difference in the culture and in the educational problem (rural life vs. city ghetto, for example) to make the book very stimulating, and I think it will be a rare reader who does not find his mind stretched by contemplating the educational boldness of people working many decades in the past. Both their successes and their mistakes are thought provoking.

The author sets this whole phenomenon in a carefully documented context of humanistic psychology as it exists in this country today. I believe this clarifies its significance for today's educators. It is a valuable contribution to the humanizing and improvement of our educational policies.

Carl R. Rogers

La Jolla, California
March, 1971

---

[2] Dillon, J. T. *Teaching High School in a Freer Fashion.*
[3] Kline, L. W. *Education and the Personal Quest.*
[4] Rogers, C. R. *Freedom to Learn.*
All published in the series, Studies of the Person, Charles E. Merrill Publishing Company, Columbus, Ohio.

PREFACE

This book has grown out of my long involvement with the folk highschools and a more recent one with the humanistic movement in psychology. I came to know the folk highschools before I began teaching, when I went to Denmark in 1954 to study education at the University of Copenhagen. I had decided I wanted to be a teacher, but had been so uninspired by the education courses I took as an undergraduate in one of California's colleges, that I felt I needed an infusion of new ideas, or air, or blood, if I were to go into teaching with the enthusiasm the job needed. I hoped that I could get that infusion in Denmark.

As it turned out, I was more rewarded than I had imagined I could be. My encounter with the folk highschools, my close contact with them, gave me a glimpse of an approach to education which was unique and exciting, fun and interesting, where the students really became inspired through their educational experience. The fact of that educational experience stayed with me through the ensuing years as I taught in various elementary schools, years during which I wondered what the folk highschool experience really meant to us here in education in this country. I read many articles wherein the authors tried to deal with this same question. The question was usually phrased in terms such as "Can the folk highschool be transplanted to the U.S.?" The fact of the matter is that highschools *have* been started in this country, but with one or two exceptions have not flourished in our soil. Transplantation, then, seemed to be out, and none of those concerned with bringing the highschool experience to young people in this country, including myself, seemed able to come up with any other suggestions. The question remained unanswered. The experience which the folk highschools offered, exciting and meaningful as it was, seemed somehow destined to remain foreign to this country.

It was only when increasing numbers of students began to demand a more relevant, human-centered education that the inklings of an answer to the question "What can the folk highschool mean for us?" began to take form. When the students began setting up their own experimental colleges and free universities, and humanistic psychology began presenting us with empirical evidence of man's drive toward coherence and meaning, his motivation toward learning and self-fulfillment, it became ever more clear the extent to which education as we knew it was failing the students—indeed, the society as a whole. The need for a change in our basic philosophy, structure, goals and methods of education is increasingly apparent.

What direction should that change take, and would it be able to encompass the philosophy and methods of the folk highschool? Humanistic psychology was telling us that man was not basically evil, a beast to be tamed at all costs, but that given a supportive, nurturing environment, tended to develop naturally in ways which we characterize as "good." It was this tendency which Carl Rogers made use of in his non-directive, client-centered therapy, where it was the patient's (or client's) own inner urge toward completeness, coherence, and meaning which provided the direction and movement in therapy, instead of the traditional therapist's judgment and "wisdom." It seemed to me that these tendencies in the "new" man were the same ones which must have prompted thousands of young people over the years to attend the folk highschools, where they got no economic reward, where they got neither diplomas nor grades, where the only outcome—the one which attracted them to the schools—was greater awareness of themselves, their abilities, and their intimate relationship to the people and the world around them.

I thought I discerned a connection between the folk highschool experience and the lessons it offered us, and this new movement toward emphasizing the human qualities inherent in man, a movement which included both the students and the humanistic psychologists. As I had taken a couple of years off from teaching to work on a doctorate, I decided to investigate the connection between these two movements to see how much they could benefit from each other. This book is one of the results of that study.

BUT WHY NOW?

In the early 1920s, American educators discovered the Danish folk highschool (which had been around since 1850). Several very enthusiastic books were written and published, articles appeared, Scandinavian-American exchanges were set up so that American teachers and students could experience first-hand the highschool experience. Excitement, as the saying goes, ran high. Then it began to ebb, lessening with each passing year, until during the past decade, virtually no mention of the Danish folk highschools could be found in the journals published in this country. Today it is a rare educator—and I mean "professional" educators, who assume responsibility for determining policies and curricula for our schools —who is aware that there is such a thing as a folk highschool.

In the recent past no one was interested in hearing about the folk highschools, the "schools for farmers." We had, after all, successfully repudiated the Progressive education movement, with its concentration on the needs of the learner. That movement and its prophet Dewey, though they may still have been enshrined in the teachers' colleges, had been effectively exorcised where it really counted: in the schools. We were interested in "quality education," in "excellence," in teaching young people things that mattered, and doing it in a rigorous manner. There was no room for such a fuzzy-headed concept as that which was behind the folk highschools. Education for self-fulfillment or enlivenment was, frankly, not in the American tradition. Then, with Sputnik we were presented with seemingly irrefutable evidence of what many had been warning us of all along. We had been coddling our young people, had been neglecting to teach them the subjects and skills which were so crucially necessary for survival in the world: mathematics, physics and chemistry. At this point studying subjects merely because you wanted to study them was more out of place than ever. The goal of self-fulfillment or enlivenment was even more fuzzy-headed; was probably tainted with subversiveness, perhaps even domination by a foreign power.

The past several decades, then, have not been the most fertile time in which to suggest that the goal of education should be the humanization of the person, his development as an individual. It has only been for a few years that the great failure of our traditional order of values has been seriously questioned by large numbers of concerned people. It is only recently that we have really begun to see the damage inflicted on our young people by our schools, the damage inflicted on the peoples of the world by our inability to learn cooperation, the damage inflicted on our planet by our blind economics of plunder. It is this growing awareness of the other side of the coin of progress, coupled with the work of a group of philosophers and psychologists who have dared to flaunt tradition and who have shown us man in a new way, which has helped to generate a climate in which a book of this kind is not only acceptable, but, I hope, may even be useful.

I would like to acknowledge the interest which Carl Rogers and William Coulson, the editors of this Series, showed in my dissertation, and their suggestion that I make it into a book. This interest is another evidence of their growing concern with the role of education, and their belief that it is through the humanistic utilization of the potential of our educational apparatus that the present careering voyage of society, hellbent for destruction, can be reversed, if at all.

I also want to acknowledge the indispensable aid of my wife, Dorothy. She encouraged, criticized, suggested. She read every page—most in several drafts, pointing out weak points, and urged me onward when my spirit flagged. Truly, without her help this book would never have come into being.

David C. L. Davis

Cazadero, California
March, 1971

CONTENTS

These schools are called Highschools because they deal with things of high concern in the life of the community; and they are called People's Highschools because they are related to the whole life of the people and those things, only, which are important to all the people. Their aim is the creation of a popular national culture which will ramify out into whatever special interest may be found in human nature, but which in its fundamentals is homogeneous and the possession of all. The path to this goal is by way of the education of personality: only through the inner freedom of personality can such a culture develop.

In order to secure this high sense of common living, the individual must be freed from the stifling constraints of the mass: he must come to know himself as a self-directing person. Therefore, inner freedom is the highest law of these schools: they do not breed submission or regimentation of spirit, but they teach the comradeship of all in the life of the community. In a word, the spirit of these schools is the spirit of democracy. It stands, therefore, in opposition to both the current popular opinion of our times and to that doctrine of the overlordship of the state in the midst of which we have been but lately living and whose form, now broken, lies behind us.

Hollman, *Die Volkshochschule,*
Paul Parey, Berlin, 1919.

1

What Is a Folk Highschool?

Since so few Americans have even heard of the Danish folk high-schools, we must settle several points at the outset. The first is the name. In Danish they are called *folkehøjskoler*. In a literal translation, this becomes *people's highschools*. However, in the United States we have no people's highschools, so the name becomes meaningless. As a consequence, I prefer, as do most others writing in English about the schools, to call them folk highschools. Of course, we don't have folk highschools in the United States, either, but the term has at least the advantage of preserving the flavor of the original for us. A second point: these are folk *high*schools, schools for older people, not folk schools. Folk schools in Denmark are what we call public schools. A folk highschool is just not a public school. It is a highschool, and this is usually the term used to describe them in Denmark. Thus: *folk highschool* or *highschool;* never folk school. Also, to keep the distinction between the folk highschool and our own high school as clear as possible, I will always spell the former as one word (as it is in Danish) and the latter as two (as it is in English).

All right, then. What *is* a folk highschool? Tolstoy said that real education "begins with a question in the life of the learner." I would say that in a very real sense a folk highschool is a place where that kind of an education is offered. It is obvious that Tolstoy's definition does not apply to public schools, either in this country or in Denmark, for we know that the questions there usually come from the teacher's book. We don't, ordinarily, go to public schools because there is a question in our lives; we go because we are supposed to. The fact is, though, that that is precisely the reason most students go to a folk highschool. They might not express it in those exact words, but it must be true, because of one of the basic facts about the highschools: they offer no diplomas, grades, certificates of completion or employment service. Neither do they have entrance requirements or atten-

3

dance requirements. One doesn't have to attend—he gets no rewards if he does. With a school like this, I can think of only one reason to attend, and that is something that might be described as "a question in the life of the learner." This was precisely the idea in the mind of the man whose idea gave birth to the folk highschool movement, Bishop N. F. S. Grundtvig. A remarkable Dane who lived at the same time as Kierkegaard, Grundtvig believed that education would only be meaningful when it spoke to a need from the learner's experience. Therefore, he thought of his school as being for young men (no women then) eighteen or over, who had some experience with life and therefore some questions about it.

The folk highschools are boarding schools, where anyone over the age of eighteen may come, irrespective of economic condition or educational background; where there is a close relationship between students and staff; and where the concern is with cultural and social problems of universal interest—which means first of all that they must be of interest to the student. These schools exist outside the regular school system by design, for only thus are they able to maintain the flexibility which enables their courses to continue to reflect the interests and concerns of their students. Their concern is not so much with the intellectual growth of the student as with his growth in a wider sphere, one which contains the intellectual but is not defined by it. The intellect is seen as only a part of the person, developing as he seeks to answer questions life has put to him, and as he seeks to discover just where he fits into the world of people and processes.

Perhaps an example from outside the folk highschool will help to make clearer what it is the highschool offers, and why students elect to attend. I have a friend, a psychologist, who teaches several classes in psychology at an adult school. Since he doesn't like to lecture, the classes are in reality discussions about the lives and concerns of the class members, with my friend furnishing a psychological orientation to the discussions—providing material for the intellectual growth of the class, for example, with background, insights, new ways of looking at things—and through his experience in counseling helping to provide movement and direction to the discussions. Recently the members of one of his classes petitioned the school to change the class from two units to three, so they could meet twice a week instead of once. Now why would these people, adults, for the most part not interested in diplomas or units, voluntarily commit themselves to a heavier class schedule than required when ostensibly they are getting nothing in return? Why, when the class session ends, does the majority of its members merely shift location to a nearby coffee shop and continue for another hour?

The reason, it seems to me, is that they *are* getting something from the class—I daresay for some of them far more than they have gotten from any other class in school. What they are getting is answers to questions put to them by life. They are getting a chance to talk seriously about what is really important to them: themselves, their relationships with others, and the problems of living. They are doing it in a learning atmosphere where new information is available to them in their attempt to deal with the questions. Thus, the class sessions are not idle chit-chat or bull-sessions. They are learning; but they are learning about things that matter. Perhaps for the first time they are experiencing learning as trying to answer *their* questions, questions which are important, vital to them, rather than trying to answer questions from the teacher, which neither he nor they really give a damn about.

I suggest that this is real education. It is not what traditional education is about, but it is what the experimental colleges are about; it is what the free universities are about; it is what the folk highschools are about, and have been for over a century. Is the adult school, then, in the case of my friend's class, a folk highschool? No, for while it possesses part of the folk highschool concept, it lacks several other characteristics. To it would have to be added the residential feature of the highschools, for out of this grows one of the most important consequences of the highschool education: a sense of community, of sharing and of trust of one's fellow students and teachers. This is just not possible to the same degree outside of a residential situation, where one shares meals, classes, free time activities, and often quarters, with one's classmates. Out of the fusion of these two aspects, the meaningful education and the growth of community, comes the highschool experience, an experience which I believe is unique in the world of education.

The other point at which my friend's class differs from a folk highschool is that of intent. The adult school does not intend to offer the kind of educational experience which my friend offers. This is clear from the negative response of the school's administrators toward what he is doing. The intent of the administrators of the folk highschool is precisely to provide this kind of meaningful education—though not all would do it in the same manner as my friend. In reality, not all highschools come equally close to achieving this ideal. There may be some, in fact, where my friend's teaching methods and philosophy would arouse as much consternation as at the adult school. There is, however, the basic intent to provide the educational experience which Grundtvig envisioned.

The first folk highschool was started in 1844 with twenty students. By 1910 there were eighty-three schools with 5600 students. Thereafter, the number of schools declined, then leveled off between 1920 and 1960 at between fifty-five and sixty schools. There are currently approximately seventy highschools. New schools are founded, some old ones close their doors, but the number has remained about the same. During this period, the school population has continued to grow and today there are more than 8500 students attending highschools yearly, which is approximately ten percent of the young people in the twenty-year-old age bracket. Though their influence on the life of the Danish nation has been large, the folk highschools have never directly involved the majority of the Danish people. At the peak of their growth, probably a third of the rural population of Denmark was attending or had attended a folk highschool. Today, while the percentage of town and city dwellers attending has increased, the majority of students still come from the country and small towns. There has been a steady rise in the number of students over the past several decades, reflecting the increase in population during that time.

The Danish Folk Highschool Act, which provides for government grants and assistance to highschools, and defines the few government standards, does not, like the corresponding Swedish, Norwegian and Finnish acts, contain a specific definition of what a highschool is. Thus, the Danish folk highschool, though it exists and is recognized by the government, is not defined by that government. It would be a mistake, however, to assume therefrom that the people in the government who propose and approve the laws do not have an idea of what one is. The fact is that highschool people have numbered among members of the government since the first days of the schools. The present principal of Magleaas Folk Highschool is a member of parliament. The principal of Krogerup Highschool at the time I stayed there was the husband of the Minister of Religion, Bodil Koch. The present Minister for Folk Highschools in the Ministry of Education is a former principal of Askov Highschool. In fact, it has been the custom—except for a short period—for the Minister of Education for Folk Highschools and Agricultural schools to be a highschool man.

This easy relationship between the government and the highschools, which has existed with only short lapses down through the years, has had much to do with the great influence which the highschools and the highschool idea have exerted on the life of the country. With highschool people and people friendly to the highschool in government and among the leaders in the voting populace, it was possible for the schools to keep their freedom which is so essential to their work and to have this freedom honored by the government. At the same time these folk highschool people carried their highschool way of thinking into matters of government with them, so that ideas of cooperation, social welfare, conservation and the like were congenial to them. Thus the highschools, thriving in the supportive climate which their graduates and supporters helped provide, were able to expose more young people to this same folk highschool idea—these people then moving out into the society and endeavoring to put the ideas into action.

I have found over the years that the task of attempting to define a folk highschool briefly is a difficult one. These schools are many things at once. A folk highschool is not only the school itself and its curriculum but also the students and why they come and what they do when they leave; at the same time it is Grundtvig's ideas and the influence the highschools have had on the Danish society. As soon as one begins to speak of one aspect of the schools, he is immediately carried on to another which is intimately connected with it. In attempting to describe what a folk highschool *is*, one may find himself also talking about many other things. In discussing the lack of an official definition of a folk highschool, one is led naturally into the relationship between the highschools and the Ministry of Education and to the fact that many former students and some teachers and principals are members of the government, or to the tradition that the Minister for Folk Highschools and Agricultural Schools is a highschool principal.

Of course, this transactional aspect of a definition of the folk highschool is natural, since a great deal of what the highschool is has to do with its organismic nature and with the fact that it not only concerns itself with the "whole" person, but with the "whole" society. One of the aims of the schools is to confirm the students' solidarity with the milieu from which they came, and to enable them when they return to make this same milieu richer and more meaningful. The highschools never divorced themselves from life, the ongoing life of their students. Describing them is in a way describing a way of life.

Yet, there must be a framework upon which to hang the flesh of the school, a framework which is important to an understanding of the organic highschool. Boiled down to the essentials, a highschool must contain the following four ingredients:

(1) It must be a boarding school. One of the essential qualities of the highschool is the close association of the students and staff (including non-teaching employees such as kitchen workers, etc.). Students and teachers and principal spend as much time together as possible. It is customary at all highschools for the teachers—and usually their families—to take their meals together with the students in the dining room.

(2) The school must provide at least one five-month course, or two lasting three months, annually. Thus we have the first two features of the highschool: that it is a boarding school and that the term is a short one compared with colleges or other boarding-type schools. Most students participate in only one term at a highschool, though many, who are able, return—often to a different school —for a subsequent term. Askov, the Extended Highschool, offers one and two year courses, but it is the main exception to the five-month rule. There are also shorter courses for various periods, many of them offered in the summers. The summer courses, being shorter, are often more experimental. Some schools offer summer sessions for families, or for older people on pensions, in an attempt to make the highschool experience available to—since in theory it is applicable to—all age groups. The schools are coeducational,

though this was not always the case. Originally, the winter term was for men while later schools set up short summer courses for women. Coeducational courses were not instituted until 1945!

(3) The school admits students belonging to all social classes and educational backgrounds. There are no educational prerequisites and, with the government grants which are available, no economic ones. In the early days the students came disproportionately from the homes of the better-off farmers, solely because it was these people who could afford to send their sons for a winter at a highschool. However, as this fact became evident, there was pressure to get government subsidies for the more needy students, and from the earliest years the schools received small subsidies.

(4) The most important part of the curriculum is concerned with cultural and social problems of universal interest. From the beginning, the two most common lines in the highschool were history and literature. After this came natural science, treated historically, music and recreation. The curriculum from the school started by Kristen Kold at Ryslinge in 1850, illustrates the central concerns of the early schools:

Great Trends in Human History
Great Themes from Biblical History
History of Christianity and the Church
Myths of the North and Denmark
Geography
Outstanding Literature of Denmark
Songs and Singing

To be sure, the curriculum today is not so simple, and the concerns are broader. Some courses have fallen by the way (Danish History, Christian History and themes, Natural Science, are examples) and others have taken their places. Since most of the new additions cannot be fitted into the schedule as regular classes, they are offered as free electives or special interest classes which meet in the afternoon or evenings. In this way the range of offerings is limited only by the qualifications of the teachers and the desires of the students.

At Askov Folk Highschool, besides the standard subjects, there are both short- and long-term special classes. The short-term classes meet three hours a week for half the term, at which time new choices are made. The long-term classes also meet three hours a week, but for the whole term. Recently the following subjects were available at Askov as long- or short-term special classes:

Short term: interior decoration; the work of the United Nations; psychology; China's old culture; musicianship; ceramics; Latin American history; masterpieces of dramatic art; problems of education and child-raising; Africa; the novel today; classic Danish literature; the culture of India; industrialism; folk tales; school and society; main currents of Danish history; spiritual currents in Denmark in the last centuries; German literature after 1945; child psychology; ancient European culture; James Joyce's *Ulysses;* turning points in the history of the Danish church.

Long term: Danish cultural history; world politics; weaving; contemporary political ideas; the recent history of natural science; bible studies; the history of philosophy; phases in the history of European civilization; politics and literature; modernism and its forerunners; Christianity; main currents in today's art.

Of course, Askov is not a typical highschool because it tends to attract to its extended course the more sophisticated students and those with a fuller educational background. However, many of its students could easily be called typical highschool students. From Askov's rich bill of fare we could go to schools where the special interest classes might number half a dozen at most, and probably classes in the arts and crafts would be in greatest demand.

It is worth noting that in the long list of elective offerings at Askov, out of forty-five classes the students can choose from, there is only one with a purely scientific emphasis. Science, which was the most popular subject before and during the first world war, has lost its attraction. At the beginning of the twentieth century, it looked as though it might be science which would bring about man's salvation, his elevation above the degrading aspects of his life. Today it is the political, social, psychological and literary questions which occupy the mind of youth, at least the mind of highschool youth: questions about *man.*

In summary, the folk highschools are boarding schools, where the students attend for five-month sessions in the winter, or shorter sessions at other times; where there is a close relationship between the students and staff which is encouraged by the very physical setup of the schools; where anyone may come, irrespective of age (as long as they have reached eighteen), economic condition or educational background; and where the concern is with cultural and social problems of universal interest.

One of the by-products of this approach to education, of course, is that in such an atmosphere new questions arise in the mind of the learner in the process of trying to find answers to the old ones; in this way the process of education really becomes open-ended. The young person (or the person of any age) who goes to the highschool searching for answers to questions which life has put to him finds in dealing with these questions that there are more which he did not have when he came. To the extent that the process continues, the student leaves his highschool experience with more questions than he arrived with, thus beginning a process which can lead to the only meaningful education, self-education. A former student, in writing of his experiences, relates that in their conversations the students talked of "the great things which we would still have time to do in this life, and in the sphere that was to be ours." Since education does not stop at the schoolhouse door, nor on graduation day, self-education is the only way one can become educated. Education must be a life-long activity; this activity is one which seems to characterize most former highschool students. The experience of finding that questions lead to questions, that the more one discovers the more there is to be discovered, is one of the ways into self-education.

Besides the four above, there are other characteristics of the folk highschools which should be emphasized: the importance given to group singing; the matter of students attending of their own will; the essential blending of fellowship and scholarship; the absence of entrance or leaving examinations; the special role and requirements for teachers. All of these are part of what makes a folk highschool what it is.

Grundtvig knew the importance of music—group singing—in establishing rapport within a group. The church, of course, has long made use of this knowledge. He also knew, from his own experience as a child, that it is a very effective educational medium. Throughout their history the highschools have laid great stress on music, especially singing. The day starts off with morning song, for instance, at which everyone is expected to be present. At that time several songs from the highschool songbook are sung and often the principal will make any announcements for the day. At some schools each class begins with the singing of a song or two, though this is usually the prerogative of the teacher.

The custom may seem strange to us, but I found in my own experience that there really was a much stronger feeling of camaraderie and being together after singing a couple of songs than there was before. The custom is so widespread in Denmark and the other Scandinavian countries that in the public schools the students meet in the assembly hall—usually between their first and second periods—for morning song. To be sure, not all of them sing, but I was always amazed at the large number who did take part—by far the majority. It is also interesting that the songbooks, both in the highschools and in the public schools, do not contain the music to the songs. This means that most Danish school children come to know a large number of songs by heart through their growing years. It was always amazing to me to hear, as one of the more than three hundred songs from that book with only words was announced, all those young people unhesitatingly singing out that tune which remained hidden from me.

Of course this is changing, even as young people today are more into music and are making it more a part of their lives. The young people of today are less willing to accept the songs of their elders without question, and with time we may see singing in the highschools take on a different appearance. The songs in the highschool songbooks (and by songs is usually meant poems, which are sung to traditional tunes), a quarter of which were written or adapted by Grundtvig himself, have over the years spoken to something in the young people who sang them, and it is quite unlikely that they will all be abandoned. Yet, over half the songs are over one hundred years old, and the songbooks owe a great deal to the nineteenth century poets and attitudes, and it may be that many of them will not say anything to the young people of today. It may be that in order to retain the use of song as an integral part of the highschool experience, new songs will have to take the place of those which are no longer relevant. Such a thing would not be too sacreligious, though, considering that many of the songs which have the longest tradition are ones that Grundtvig himself adapted from others' work. And, of course, he wrote a great number himself—precisely for the reason that he felt they needed to be relevant to the times.

Grundtvig wrote that for teachers for his proposed highschool he wanted men who loved what they were teaching: "One ... who knew and loved the history of the Fatherland and could talk about it so interestingly that the young people will become excited by it." He saw the need for the young people to see a subject as being important and relevant enough to take up a person's whole time. The teacher must also be someone the student could respect as a person; a person first, a teacher second. The highschool teacher's role is not to lay before the students the subject matter, which he will then require them to reproduce back to him. His task, rather, is to attempt, through his own life experiences—which include the subject matter he has made his—to awaken them to an interest in and a commitment to life. At the same time he attempts to show them new ways to look at life.

He participates in the free-time activities of the students, trying to make their stay a fruitful whole. He will discover soon that the line between teaching hour and other activities is difficult to draw, and when he has gotten some experience "he will realize that there is no advantage in drawing it," as the present Minister for Highschools and Agricultural Schools wrote in an article to teachers-to-be. That which takes place spreads over work and free time, holy and secular, and cannot be enclosed in any single area.

Teaching credentials, degrees or diplomas are not necessary for a highschool teacher. What is necessary is a strong desire to be a highschool teacher, ability or experience in some area which will be useful to the students—the core courses still include Danish, foreign languages, physical education, mathematics, science, and similar subjects—and a desire to share that ability or experience with young people. The pay is not great—it has been increased recently to approximate that of public school teachers—and the work load is large. Officially a full-time teacher's load is six hundred hours yearly. However, a recent survey disclosed that the average highschool teacher's load was closer to 720 than 600. Added to that was an additional two hundred hours or more of "other educational work" such as setting up tours, theater per-

formances, entertainments, demonstrations, etc. On top of that is
the informal contact with the students which at a boarding school
can take up a great deal of time.

The following is an extract from a teacher's contract with a
folk highschool, circa 1947. This was a small school. Probably at a
larger school the teacher's duties would be fewer.

> The duties of the position are as follows: teaching 20–25 les-
> sons per week, of these 6–12 will be lecture classes. He shares with
> the principal the arrangement and supervision of all festivities and
> meetings, as also everything regarding the repair of rooms and
> equipment. He must be willing to keep up telephone connections
> with artisans and tradespeople. He is entrusted with the daily su-
> pervision of the students, their rooms, and the classrooms, as also
> the students' return in time after Sundays and holidays, and their
> proper use of heating, lighting, water, and gymnastic appliances,
> etc. He is in duty bound, except on his weekly day off and free
> evening, both on Sundays and weekdays to be present at all the
> school's meals, just as his wife and children are normally supposed
> to take part in them, with the sole exception of breakfast.
>
> It must be particularly emphasized that he, as well as the prin-
> cipal and other masters, must consider it an essential part of his
> duty to keep an open house for both present and former students,
> both individually and in groups. It goes without saying that his
> private family life and the preparation for his classes will to some
> extent limit these activities. However, there are three rules which
> can in no way be abrogated:
>
> 1) He, his wife, and their home must on Sundays, and especially
> Sunday evenings, always be at the disposal of the students. It must
> be regarded by them as a matter of course, in a couple of evening
> hours, to receive them or to take part in their gatherings in the
> school-rooms. They must be prepared also to give up part of the
> day to gatherings or arrangements for the amusement of the young,
> and this must take first place before, or be compatible with, the
> reception of private guests. This is what the weekly day off is for.
> The teacher, or teacher's wife, who is not willing to make this sac-
> rifice for the calling, should not apply for the position.
>
> 2) At least on two other evenings every week some time should
> be set aside for short visits from pupils and interviews with them.
>
> 3) To old pupils, arriving from afar, the doors must be kept as
> widely open as possible. Keeping up good relations with them is a
> particularly important part of the task.[1]

[1] Thomas Rørdam, *The Danish Folk Highschools* (Copenhagen, Denmark:
Det Danske Selskab, 1965), p. 34.

As I say, the duties at a larger highschool might not be so all-embracing, but the tone of the contract and the terms exemplify what it is that a folk highschool teacher is expected to do and be (and his wife, also). It is no place for the misanthrope or the person who can only take his students in small doses. At the same time, for one who enjoys social contacts with students and other teachers, it can be a stimulating and exciting experience.

That the students come to the highschool of their own free will (sometimes aided by that of their parents) is important both to the philosophy of the school and the carrying out of its goals. The fact that the students are there, and not there for a diploma or degree, suggests that they are interested in what the highschool can offer them. Most are well aware of the nature and emphasis of the schools. As a consequence, the teacher is reasonably sure that there is an interest in what he has to offer.

Once they get to the school, students will find varying degrees of freedom of action, depending on the school they choose. Some schools are still operating in the old tradition of the benevolent parent, who makes most of the decisions about studies and social behavior, leaving only certain areas for the student to exercise his freedom. A growing number of schools have bowed to the pressures of the times, and are allowing the students greater freedom of choice both in the matter of studies and social conduct. It is unrealistic to accept students who, in their home milieu were accustomed to much freedom, try to keep them sheltered while at school, and send them back to their free home environment. Even the more traditional schools are finding that they must resolve this question of the greater freedom young people have in today's society.

Whatever the amount of social freedom and freedom to choose classes, there is another freedom in the highschool which varies only slightly from school to school, and which is an integral part of the highschool idea. This is the freedom from examinations. It is manifested first of all in the fact that there are no entrance examinations or school-leaving examinations. In a country which, in the European tradition, is rife with examinations, where they are encountered at all levels and to a great degree determine one's school experiences and employment opportunities, a non-examination school is a radical departure.

We in the U.S. do not have examinations like those in the European countries—comprehensive, "external" (administered by authorities from outside the individual school), year end, and "school-leaving" examinations, which purport to test the student on everything he has learned up to the point of the examination and which, in a very real sense, can determine the student's future, as they govern admission to higher schools and determine which track the student will find himself in. It is obvious that such examinations effectively control the curriculum in the schools. Each teacher is free to teach pretty much as he wishes—in one public school I visited the three teachers of English each used a different textbook series and different methods. However, the comprehensive exams—administered not by the teacher but by an external board of examiners—means that all teachers must cover essentially identical material if they do not want to jeopardize their students' chances. The only teacher in the public schools who is free of this limitation is the one who teaches the least academically able students—those who plan to leave school at the earliest opportunity.

One of the reasons the folk highschools have been able to be innovative and have been able to fit their curricula to the changing times is that there is no examination controlling what they teach and when. Another advantage at least as important is that lacking examinations, tests, or grades, the teacher is required to approach the areas of discipline and subject matter in a non-traditional way. When one has grades or examinations as weapons, one can often force students to conform to behavior patterns which they do not accept. Likewise, by the use of grades one can sometimes force them to "learn" subject matter which does not appear relevant to them, at speeds which are not of their own choosing. In the absence of grades and tests as a coercive tool, the teacher is left with the major motivational tool of the highschool teacher— the students' interest. When the students are interested in what is going on and when they feel that it is important, the problem of discipline and learning becomes less crucial. In this respect it is important to recognize that the student's decision to attend or not to attend means that in general the highschool does not have the problem of disinterested students being forced to attend against their will.

Comradeship and scholarship go together at a highschool. There is no attempt at a highschool to subordinate the student's social and emotional growth to his intellectual growth. Each is a valid part of the student and his development and, in fact, the social growth is essential to the type of educational experience offered at the highschool. Grundtvig, when he visited Cambridge University, was impressed by the quality of the social life there. He saw that the communal living and eating, the discussions and get-togethers among the students, the sharing of the social life, were as important to the quality of the education they got as the subject matter they learned. In fact, much of what constituted a "Cambridge education" was a result of this very communal social life at the school.

Therefore, when he formulated his ideas for a folk highschool for the North, he made sure of a place in the school for this side of education, through the school being a boarding school and by arranging it so that there were large amounts of time when the students did not have to be studying or attending lectures. By also emphasizing the being-together of the students and the teachers, he tried to ensure that the interaction would be "enlightening" besides being "enlivening." In all respects, Grundtvig felt that it was the living aspects of the school which were important; the interplay among ideas, the interaction among students and teachers, the concern with the questions put by life. This is also the reason for his emphasis on the lecture—the "living word" as he called it. There is a great difference between reading about history from a book, for example, and hearing the story from someone for whom the incidents live and matter, and who can bring them living to the students. It is likely that those who have had lecture courses in school carry with them a picture of a lecturer quite different from the one Grundtvig had. The lecturer Grundtvig had in mind was far from the one who reads monotonously from notes already read a hundred times, or rambles boringly, failing utterly to involve the students. He was more akin to a bard or storyteller, someone who could enthrall his listeners with his tales, one who could bring to life the subject he was talking about, one who involved his audience. For the living word, as Grundtvig saw it, was not a one way process—though too often it has been so interpreted by many of his followers—but required participation and interaction with the students, the listeners. This was the lecture he proposed for the highschool, from which the students would go out brimming with questions and ideas and with new vistas opened to them. At this point it was important to have the time to gather and discuss the ideas and questions which the lecture had generated, and to have the teachers available, so that the dialogue could continue outside the classroom.

Thus, with all the emphasis on fellowship and being together, the sharing of experiences requires experiences to share. At the highschool, these shared experiences ideally come from the lectures and classes and they provide the stuff of the informal discussions and the basic material for widening the students' outlook. Without this fuel, the discussions and get-togethers would offer little that the students could not get in their home environments. The participation by the students in lectures and classes helps to create the feeling of shared experience which is a prerequisite for comradeship and community.

The influence which the highschools have had on the Danish society has been remarked by many. Among those foreigners who have written about them, the schools are given credit for much of what is good in Denmark: the cooperative movement, the high level of literacy, the success of the Danish farmer in competing in the world market, the advanced social legislation. Danes, too, are generally agreed that the highschools deserve a large part of the credit for many of the features that characterize Denmark and the Danish way of life, though at the same time they caution against the assumption that the highschools have done it all.

Most of those who have studied the highschool movement are in agreement that the impetus for the cooperative movement, especially as it exists in Denmark, came from the highschools and the experience in cooperative living which their students acquired. Peter Manniche, who founded the International People's College at Elsinore, a Folk Highschool, writes of the differences between the Swedish and Danish cooperatives. The original Danish cooperatives were based on the idea of *joint responsibility*—the idea that all are responsible for the debts of any member. This is an idea which would be highly unlikely to occur in a situation where the members did not trust one another. As Manniche points out, the Swedish cooperatives and the later consumer cooperatives which were established in the towns and cities in Denmark were *limited liability* companies, where one's trust toward his fellow need not necessarily be so great.[2] Another aspect of the Danish farmers' cooperatives is that they grew spontaneously. The cooperatives came first, out of the farmers' needs, and the theory came second. They were not established as the result of a theory.

In a competitive society, the failure of your neighbor can mean your own success. Cooperation, however, can only be carried forward by people who are ready to share their successes and failures with others. It is this spirit of fellowship, of readiness to share, which the folk highschools helped to foster. At the same time, it must be pointed out that cooperation was not one of the subjects in the highschool, which brings us back to the point made by Manniche, that the cooperative movement grew out of an experience which the people had at the highschools, not out of any theory they learned. Today over eighty percent of the farmers in Denmark are members of one or more cooperative associations, some being in as many as a dozen different purchasing and selling societies.

Though there are those who caution care in assigning to the highschools credit for whatever is good in Danish culture, and others who would deny them any value whatsoever, there are others who are more enthusiastic. The question of who is right— or who is more right—is probably impossible to decide. Indeed, it may be merely a matter of one's taste. After all, it is impossible to return and start again in order to obtain a control group. And it may well be that the important factor was that Denmark was a small and homogeneous country, as some have suggested. However, there are other small, homogeneous countries which have not attained the level of equality and social consciousness coupled with a literacy which is quite remarkable. If one believes with George Russell that a nation is cultivated only insofar as the average man, not the exceptional person, is cultivated and has knowledge of the thought, imagination, and intellectual history of his nation and to some extent has an awareness of the rest of the

---

[2] Peter Manniche, "Farmers' Cooperatives in Denmark," in *Adult Education in the Struggle for Peace,* ed. Peter Manniche (Copenhagen, Denmark: G. E. C. Gads Forlag, 1949), p. 90.

world, then Denmark must be known as a cultivated nation. If one includes in the criteria for a cultivated nation a high degree of social responsibility coupled with a respect for the individual's freedom, then, again, Denmark must be included. As far as the folk highschool's responsibility for this condition is concerned, an appraisal can only be based on three things: the reports of concerned parties—former students, including farmers, teachers, writers, bankers, board chairmen, government officials, clerks, salesgirls, etc.; similarities between the goals and methods and philosophy of the highschools on the one hand, and conditions in the society on the other—especially changes in the society which parallel the goals of the highschools; and finally, one's own evaluation, either of the folk highschool experience if one has participated in it (as in my own case), or evaluation of the other two types of data.

While I believe it would be foolish to give the highschool movement credit for everything good in Danish society, I also believe that through interaction with the society, the highschool movement and Grundtvig's philosophy (which also reached the people through the pulpit, his pamphlets and books, and his participation in the government) and that of others of a like mind, came to have an important effect on the Danish society, an effect which influenced it in the direction of a more humanistic approach to the problems of human life in the industrial age. Joseph K. Hart, writing of the folk highschools and the Danes in 1927 had this to say:

> The people have slowly *made up their minds* to control the conditions of their living, and to make the machinery of life subordinate to the spirit of life . . .[3]

A couple of examples from my own experience exemplify for me this humanistic emphasis on the spirit of life over the machinery. Though it is becoming increasingly difficult to do in the cities, when roads are built in Denmark, bicycle paths are built alongside them. There are thousands of cyclists in Denmark. Large numbers of them cycle to work and back. Families vacation on bicycles. One of the major reasons they can do so is that on all but the nar-

---

[3] Joseph Hart, *Light from the North* (New York: Henry Holt and Company, 1927), p. 61.

rowest streets in the cities, and on all the new roads traversing the countryside, there are paved bicycle paths separated from the automobile lanes. They could have been left out; they are certainly not a feature of road-building plans in most countries. They may have nothing whatsoever to do with folk highschools, and they too, may fall victim to the advancing automobile and petroleum monster, but up till now it is an example in microcosm of the Danish approach to life, the concern for the small people. Another instance, also connected with bicycles, shows the same concern. At one of the lectures on Denmark which I attended while a student in Copenhagen, the speaker explained the nature of the traffic laws to us. A curious feature of the laws, especially to the motorist from the United States, was that in a collision the severity of the punishment and fine is partially dependent upon the size of the object hit. It is therefore a much more heinous crime to hit a bicyclist than to hit another car, and the fine is commensurate.

From my own experience I can well connect this Danish way of life with what I have found to be true of the folk highschool experience. The spirit of fellowship, the concern about others; these appear alike in the highschool and in the society—though to a lesser degree in the latter. Again I would like to say that it would be foolish to attribute the whole thing to the highschools or even to Grundtvig's ideas. After all, both had to exist in an environment which was congenial to them, so that what happened in Denmark *might* not have happened elsewhere. It is important to remember, though, that it has been the *interaction* between the society and the highschools which has accomplished what has been accomplished. If the folk highschool found a congenial environment, it in turn, through its graduates and their activities, helped to make that environment even more hospitable to the humanistic folk highschool ideas. The working of this transactional relationship between the schools and the society, and its importance, can be better appreciated, perhaps, by looking at the situation in the U.S. where the people, who generally hated their schools and their teachers, refuse to vote them money to operate. In addition they enact laws designed to control educators, whom they apparently regard as incompetent (just the other day someone explained to me that "Those who can, do; those who can't, teach") and untrustworthy. In California, for example, legislation was passed preventing anyone with an education major—that is, anyone whose main interest was in education and its problems—from holding an administrative or supervisory position in a school. Obviously, there were "good" reasons for passing such a law. Equally obviously the law is absurd on the face of it. One needn't go into the ramifications of refusing to allow policemen to become chiefs, soldiers to become officers, even business admistration majors to become officers in a corporation to see that. How absurd the law was is demonstrated by the fact that since it was passed there has been a steady progression of rulings whose function has been to make the law workable by making more and more exceptions to it. Also in California, a state superintendent of instruction who campaigned on a platform of mistrusting and insulting teachers was elected, again, by people who must hold some sort of grudge against teachers and schools, a grudge which in many cases is well-founded, I suspect. Looking at these two places, California and Denmark, we can see the process of interaction between the schools and the society, and the wildly disparate directions in which the process can take us.

As I write this, the schools in Los Angeles, the nation's second largest city, are paralyzed by a strike of teachers. They are demanding higher salaries, but more important they are demanding improvements in the quality of education for the children—repair of dank, crumbling buildings, an end to overcrowding in classrooms, adequate provision for sound control in the rooms, to name but a few. All the conditions are the result of one thing: lack of money. The people of the city of Los Angeles can't or won't vote enough extra taxes on themselves to pay for the school system they need. The state legislators will not or cannot find money to support impoverished school districts out of state funds. The situation has been growing steadily worse and is not limited to Los Angeles. Finally, at this juncture, the teachers have decided to defy the law and strike in an effort to dramatize the seriousness of the crisis. This much is straightforward and easy to understand. What is impossible to understand is the reaction to the teachers' action of the school board, the state legislators, the State Superintendent of Instruction and the governor. All are sworn to support free public education for all children in the state. The school board and the superintendent were ostensibly elected for that express purpose. Yet, what is their reaction to the teachers' action? To a man they have opposed the teachers. They have threatened them, vilified them, done everything but the one thing they should have done, which is to admit that a critical situation exists and that something must be done about it immediately, in concert with the teachers.

What can motivate such seemingly incomprehensible action by those who are supposed to ensure that our public school system continues to function and function in the best possible manner? I can see it only as the logical result of an approach to education which has systematically degraded and alienated generations of young people through the years; people who, now that they are adult and as voters control the purse strings to the schools, can have their revenge (though they may never think of it as such) on the teachers they disliked and the schools which made so much of their youth a time of pain and anger.

The Danish folk highschool, then, is an integral part of the Danish culture—a culture, as some believe, the highschools themselves have helped to shape. Yet, they have never directly involved over a third of the Danish population, at the most generous estimates. In Denmark, a country one third the area of Georgia with a population of about five million, there are sixty highschools, more than eight thousand students, and many hundred teachers, all engaged in an undertaking which is not calculated to benefit them materially. While the figures are small, in another sense they are provocative. The city of Los Angeles has about 500,000 school age children. Denmark has approximately the same number. When you try to imagine sixty or so small schools scattered around Los Angeles, each with 150 or less students, all of whom are eighteen or over and who share in the residential life of the school for a five-month period—not for any diploma or job skill, but merely to benefit from the learning experience—it is a little easier to see how the highschools might have had an influence on the Danish society out of all proportion to their size and numbers. Even admitting that the Danish highschools are located in rural areas and that they have never gained a foothold in the cities, can one imagine the effect of even sixty or seventy such schools, scattered throughout California's rural areas (remembering that California has a population almost four times that of Denmark) oriented to our times and ways, but still with the same humanistic goal of providing a growth experience for young people?

Of course, something very similar to that *is* taking place, in the free schools and cooperative schools, on both the elementary and secondary level, which are being started around this country. These schools are trying to achieve the goals which the folk high-schools have worked toward over the years. The free schools and cooperative schools are, in a real way, a response to and a reaction against the public schools which many parents feel are deadening their children. It may turn out that the free schools are able to take that step which in Denmark was left untaken—that of allow-ing truly free education, where each school group is autonomous and the centrally controlled and directed educational system will be replaced by organic schools which grow up around the needs of people to teach and to learn.

Let us look now at the man, N. F. S. Grundtvig, whose name is almost synonymous with folk highschool, and examine the ideas which have had such a powerful influence in Denmark.

2

The Prophet of the North

Nicolai Frederik Severin Grundtvig was born in Denmark in 1783 and died ninety years later. Poet, priest, pamphleteer, Bishop of Roskilde, gadfly, philosopher, educational revolutionary, believer in democracy, he did his part in those ninety years to keep Denmark stirred up. Though he was Bishop of Roskilde, he was at times forbidden to use the pulpit because of his radical ideas— such as freedom within the church. He was a prodigious writer, of prose and poetry. Scores of his poems are in the hymn books and school songbooks in Denmark and, though they may not be great poetry, they express a love for and belief in the people and the land. He was an indefatigable pamphleteer, exchanging verbal blows with Kierkegaard, among others.

Grundtvig was a true force for liberalization and democracy in Denmark; from the pulpit, from his position as a member of Parliament, to which he was elected when he was sixty-five, as a pamphleteer and poet, and as one who from time to time had the ear of the king. He had a strong faith in the common man and his life was spent championing him and working for his benefit. The folk highschool, for which Grundtvig's name is best known outside Denmark, was intended to be a means through which the common man could be helped to learn his own value and his strength-giving ties with his country's past and the mother tongue.

Grundtvig believed that the "living word" of the mother tongue, as he called it, had great power and meaning. At the time he lived this was quite a radical doctrine. Schooling at that time, especially beyond the elementary school, was carried out in Latin. Latin and German were spoken by the educated classes. Danish was used only by the peasants and servants and by their masters when speaking to them.

He had been through the Latin schools—he called them "black schools" and "schools for death." They taught about dead subjects, in a dead language, and they deadened the students who were forced to endure them—and he despised them. In 1854 he said categorically in his book *The Danish Folk Highschools* (1965) that "if the question came up of closing down all the grammar schools in the whole kingdom, I would vote for it."

He attended the universities of Aarhus and Copenhagen, where he studied divinity, and at the age of twenty-two he obtained a position as tutor to a family on the island of Langeland. This event turned out to be a turning point in his life, for there he fell in love with the young mother of his charge. "The most bitter scoffer of love," he wrote, "saw a woman and loved at once as greatly as it is possible to a mortal." [1] The situation being impossible, he turned to work in an attempt to derive some good out of it. He worked day and night, studying and writing. He had earlier, while at the university, heard lectures by his cousin Henrik Steffins on German Romanticism and now he turned to the new German Romantic philosophers, especially Fichte and Schelling. He read the poetry of Goethe and Schiller and the drama of Shakespeare. He became very interested in the old Norse mythology, hoping to find in it a reconciliation between the finite and the infinite. He believed that through poetry, philosophy and religion this reconciliation could be effected. He turned to poetry and began to write of the glories of the Norse past.

On his return to Copenhagen he devoted himself to a new translation into modern Danish of the Norse Sagas of Saxo and Snorre—a work which took him eight years—hoping to make this heritage available to the common people. He was concerned that the people had no connection with their cultural roots. He did not like the apathy in the nation which followed the defeat in 1814 at the hands of England when Denmark made the mistake of siding with Napoleon. The loss of Norway, which followed soon after, almost halved the land area of Denmark, and it seemed as though the country might not recover from the blow. He believed that ties with the virile past were essential to a vigorous and vital nation, especially at such a hopeless-seeming time.

In the ancient sagas of the North he saw what seemed to him such a noble philosophy of human destiny that for the rest of his life he found in them the natural source for the expression of the

---

[1] Peter Manniche, "A Brief History of Grundtvig and the Folk High School," in *Adult Education in the Struggle for Peace,* ed. Peter Manniche (Copenhagen: G. E. C. Gads Forlag, 1949), p. 95.

battles of the spirit throughout life. These myths were the themes of some of his earliest writing, both in prose and in poetry.

He believed that if the people could only come into touch with their forefathers, come into spiritual contact with them, they would be helped out of the dispiritedness and hopelessness which followed the defeat. But after translating so much of this heritage he was dismayed to discover that the common people were not reading it. Then he remembered that in his own life it had been the "living word" of his mother and an old peasant woman who had lived with them and who had told him the old legends and stories of the great deeds of his own ancestors and sung him Danish songs which had awakened in him the interest that had subsequently sent him to the history books in his father's library, there to pore over the *History of Denmark, World History* and *The Life of Luther*.

He realized that what he had been trying to do was all too similar to the very thing he had hated in the Latin school and the university—attempting to pass on a living cultural tradition, and engender a love for it, through the dead world of books. "Dead are letters," he wrote, "even if they be written with the fingers of angels, and dead is all knowledge which does not find response in the life of the reader." [2] The idea of a Danish highschool, where the people could receive the living word as he, himself, had received it began to occupy his thoughts. The school would ideally be for young men and women at the age of spiritual creation—the years beginning around eighteen when the serious and deep questions of life and its meaning were of importance.

Grundtvig felt that intellectual work is not only largely wasted on the very young but that, by denying the natural urge of children to play, experiment and be active, it is actually harmful. Further, he was convinced that until the body and brain have fully developed and until life has revealed itself so completely to the individual that he can recognize it when it is described and feel a natural desire to be enlightened, the kind of enlightenment he had in mind would fall on barren ground and be largely wasted effort. The soul of the full-grown youth is far more filled with questions

---

[2] Ibid., pp. 99–100.

than it was during the earlier years, and it would be the task of the highschool to help youth to find the answers to these questions.

When he was twenty-seven, Grundtvig came to a crisis in his religious beliefs which occasioned a brief mental breakdown. The consequence was that he turned from his mainly contemplative approach to Christianity and, in line with a new, more personal faith, decided to become a reformer. He saw himself as a judge of his own age and chastised the Danish people and men of the church for their lack of faith.

However, the more he studied the Bible the more he believed it must be interpreted, and it was obvious that the interpreters— the theologians—never agreed. At last, in 1825 at the age of forty-two, after a period of black despair brought on in part because of this dilemma, he suddenly came to the realization that Christianity had existed *before* the Bible, that it had existed among the disciples and in the living church. Christianity was not a doctrine, then, but a religious community. Its source of power was in the living aspects of the church, and in the people and the oral traditions: in the "living word."

The discovery was like a rebirth for him. There came a change in his conception of his fellow man. He discarded the dark, pessimistic, sin-centered Christianity of his reformer days and embraced the notion of the beauty and goodness of human life. Instead of exhorting man to give up his evil ways and rather than cataloguing for him his sins, Grundtvig saw as the mission of the church building on what was already positive and good in him and helping him find the way to his own enlightenment and fulfillment.

One of the consequences of Grundtvig's new view of man was his conviction that the common man must have a chance at a meaningful education. The common people, and especially the peasant children, received only the most rudimentary education.

He believed that this vital force, this "living word," which had held Christians together for over a thousand years could hold together the traditions and values of the Danish people. The medium, as he saw it, was inspired and inspiring teachers using the sagas and legends of the North to inspire the people with the strength of their own traditions and history. The "living word" was to transform the apathetic, uninformed masses into enlivened citizens.

It was also during this period that Denmark was moving toward democracy. Many of the large landowners had been granting freedom to the villeins, who had formerly been required to spend the years between fourteen and thirty-six on the estate where they were born. Adscription (the attachment of the serf to the soil) was abolished. The open field system of farming was abandoned and the tenant farmers became freeholders.

In 1831 Frederik VI, the absolute monarch, set up Farmers' Advisory Councils in the provinces. By 1841 local municipal councils were being set up and in 1848 the Constitutional Assembly began work on a plan for a constitutional monarchy.

Grundtvig and others saw in the period a great need for an access to further education for the sons of the peasants so that their participation in the newly-democratic government could be truly enlightened and they would not be at the mercy of the better educated landowners and merchants and find themselves mere pawns in the ostensible democratic processes of the new government.

Grundtvig envisioned an academy, under the protection of the king—a Royal Highschool—where the intelligent and promising sons of the farmers and workers could further their education and prepare themselves to be leaders, both in the government and among the electorate. But the school was not to be merely a watered-down version of a Latin school. It was to be a "school for life," where the students would be awakened to the beauty and value of their Nordic inheritance. They would be taught in the "mother tongue" and through great teachers would come to appreciate it and through it would come their own involvement with the stream of history and with their fellow man.

"Mother tongue" and "fatherland"—these were essential elements in Grundtvig's educational thought. These two concepts cannot have the same connotations for us today that they had for Grundtvig. "Mother tongue"—which of you reading this is in a land where you are not able to use the tongue you learned as a child, at your mother's knee, your mother tongue? Not too long ago I could have said that to all intents, with the exception of recent immigrants, no one in this country was really in that situation. Today we have suddenly realized—been forced to see—that there are many who come under that category. The Mexican-Americans, many of whom go to school where the teachers speak no Spanish, are frequently labeled as mentally retarded because the I.Q. tests are naturally in English. Indian children are sent, often against their will and the wishes of their family, to the Indian Service boarding school where they may be *forbidden* to speak their own language. And the blacks have been deprived of the use of their languages for so long that it has never occurred to most people that they had any language other than that well-known corruption of the white man's dialect by means of which they secretly made fun of the master while seeming to prove his belief that they were lazy, ignorant, happy-go-lucky. We can see the growing realization of this deprivation among blacks today who take Swahili names and study Swahili in Black Culture schools.

Even as unlikely a group as the Pilgrim Fathers strongly felt the importance of the mother tongue. One of the main reasons they left Holland—where they did, after all, have religious freedom—was because their children would have been required to attend Dutch schools, where they would have had to learn the Dutch language. This was unacceptable to them and they left Holland for friendlier linguistic climes.

If mother tongue means little or nothing to many of us today, and this includes the great majority of the people in the United States who have grown up speaking English and have not had to learn another language in order to make themselves understood in shopping, in doing business, or in order to remain abreast of current writings in their field, the same cannot be said of "fatherland." Memories of the depredations committed by the Nazis in the name of the fatherland are recent enough in the minds of many people that the term has come to be associated with imperialism and warlike nationalism. It is as though fatherland had inevitably been the excuse for a strong nation's attacks against a weaker neighbor. The word has come to have very definite negative connotations, so it may be hard to empathize with Grundtvig's concern with it. Yet we should remember that here in the United States our children sing in their classrooms "My Country 'tis of Thee" and "America the Beautiful," and that scarcely a public event begins without a singing of the national anthem and a pledge of allegiance to the flag—not even football games, boxing matches or symphonies are excepted. While we, the "melting pot of the races" are not, perhaps, accustomed to think in terms of a fatherland, there can be little doubt that the idea of "my country" is as strong here as elsewhere.

But why did Grundtvig, a Christian, a believer in the common man, and a democrat, put so much emphasis on a concept which has been the excuse for so much bloodshed and destruction? How could he make it a cornerstone for his education for life? I believe the question is worth pursuing. Part of the answer to this seeming inconsistency lies in Danish history. For many generations Denmark was engaged in a struggle to maintain its borders and its territories. The bitter conflict with Prussia (later Germany) over the duchies of Holstein and Slesvig, which were now part of the one and now part of the other nation; the loss of both Norway and Sweden, which had at one time been part of the Danish kingdom; the frivolousness of the privileged classes in Denmark, who turned toward the continent for their culture and ideas; the low esteem in which the Danish language itself was held; the fact that the nation seemed to be sinking into apathy; all these, coupled with his love for the virile Norse past, caused Grundtvig to think deeply about "fatherland" and "mother tongue." He felt strongly the necessity to return for strength to where the people had their roots.

Jørgen Bukdahl, the Danish writer, has suggested that part of the reason for Grundtvig's preoccupation with the nationalistic may be traced to the influence of the German pre-romantic, Johann Herder.[3] Herder was a philosopher of history whose ideas on nationalism were similar to Grundtvig's and predated them. It was Herder's view that the conditions necessary for a growth of a nation's spiritual life included a people's history, its legends, songs and fairy tales in which its unique qualities find expression—in all that which makes it expressly Norse, German, French or whatever. Herder stressed the importance of establishing a strong link with this past.

For Herder and for Grundtvig, the national was not an end in itself. As Bukdahl points out, "the national is never a goal of a

---

[3] Jørgen Bukdahl, "The North and Europe," in *Adult Education in the Struggle for Peace*, ed. Peter Manniche (Copenhagen, Denmark; G. E. C. Gads Forlag, 1949), p. 209.

nation's endeavors, but a condition of growth for its efforts toward
internationalism and world citizenship." [4] According to this view a
nation, like an individual, must have an identity. Bukdahl says
"You must learn to say *I* before you can say *you* or *we*." [5] Here we
can see some of the debt which Grundtvig owed to the German
Romantics, and the debt the highschool idea owes to his unre-
quited love for the beautiful Constance Leth, when he turned to
books to try to make that painful situation more bearable. For the
central concern of Romanticism is the personality. Personality
does not rest upon education, which is the solution of the Enlightenment. Rather, it is the result of a process from within, a development of the reserves, the creative potential, the urge toward
oneness. You must first be yourself; you must be in possession of
yourself—not in the sense of being self-controlled, but rather in
the sense of being aware of one's self, being open to one's self; in
Kierkegaard's words "to be that self which one truly is." You must
learn to say *I*. What you *are* is not complete or consummated until
your relationship with others is established, but that relationship,
that community, can only be established through the *I*, by one who
is able to say *I*.

This is true of human beings and, in Herder's view, is true of
nations also. In a nation the *nationalistic* corresponds to the *I*.
Only a nation which has a sense of identity—strong ties with its
roots—can afford to move out past the nationalistic stage into that
of world citizenship. A nation which has not gained a foothold in
its own culture, if it does not have a strong sense of its identity, is
stuck in the nationalistic phase. It will seek to confirm its status
by expansionism and attempts to subjugate and control weaker
neighbors. The energies which would have been used in working
past the nationalistic stage, instead are used to develop chau-
vinism, jingoism, etc. They are a substitute for self-understanding
or self-possession. [6]

It is in this view of history that I think Grundtvig's nationalism can be understood. He perceived that especially during those
years after the Great Defeat and the loss of Norway, Denmark
was in danger of losing its self-identity. His desire was to

---

[4] Ibid., p. 191.
[5] Ibid., p. 225.
[6] Ibid., p. 197.

strengthen this identity so that Denmark could take its place in the community of nations. His belief that only through the national could the nationalistic be transcended is substantiated in great part, I believe, by ensuing developments. In the early days of the highschools, Danish history, language, and culture formed the core of the curriculum. This emphasis has declined in importance over the years as a highschool subject and some schools today have dropped it entirely as a required subject and offer it, when it is offered, as an elective. Of course it could be argued that a more obvious reason for dropping it as a required subject could be that the public schools are doing a better job of teaching it, so that it is not necessary for the highschools to do so. That this line of reasoning may not be widespread can be seen, however, from our own experience. In our country the study of U.S. history is prescribed many times and in California, at least, it is a required subject in elementary school, junior high school, high school and college. The only conclusion I can draw from such an array is that educators at whatever level tend not to trust what their colleagues at other levels do, and reserve for themselves the right to do it properly. Whether folk highschool teachers are free from this tendency I do not know. Probably a stronger argument for Grundtvig's approach to nationalism is the fact that where Danish history has been dropped from the highschool curriculum its place has been taken in many instances by courses in the history of developing nations, the history of China, and courses in international relations.

I think it is also significant in discussing Grundtvig's concern with the fatherland and mother tongue that Denmark has not become an insular, nationalistic nation. The Danish people are aware of and concerned with what is happening in the wider world. Danish support of the United Nations is extremely strong. Though small and relatively powerless, it is a nation of the world.

Though Grundtvig's main concern was with a royal highschool for potential leaders, and though to his death he espoused this cause, he was not unaware of the need for a highschool for the rest of the workers and peasants. In an article published in 1838, he wrote:

> But if a Danish Highschool, as royal, as free, as much of-the-people (folkelig) as possible is necessary for the education of civil ser-

vants, should it be less necessary for the great portion of the population, who either don't want to be or can't be civil servants but who must support both themselves and the others? [7]

Grundtvig saw his school as centering around five main areas. Ideally, he wrote in an article on making Soro Academy into a Folk Highschool,[8] the school should have the following teachers:

One at least who was especially gifted in the *mother tongue*, not just as it is found in books, but as it is spoken throughout the land in all its power and variety.

One at least who both knew and loved the *fatherland's history* and could talk about it so interestingly that the young people would become excited about it. But the young people were not to be plagued with names, dates and all manner of inconsequential things, but rather should become acquainted with the great and good which have taken place in their country, which dangers it has been through and the honor it has acquired, so that they can feel what responsibilities they have for it and its future.

One at least who knew and loved the *songs of the people*, both the old and the new and who either could lead the singing or have an assistant who could. For the songs of the people are one of the best educational activities there are, at the same time that singing builds up a spirit of community among the singers.

One at least who had *traveled in the fatherland* and could tell of its cities and towns, its fields and villages, its people and their tasks, occupations and ways of thinking. For as boring for young people as geographical details and statistical tables are, just as interesting and meaningful is a living presentation on the fatherland's and people's occupations, their ways and strengths.

Finally, there should be one who knows *law*. Not one who is wrapped up in law books and statutes, but one who can inform the young people about the government's lawful basis and the general legal conditions which they will find.

This is not to say, he continues, that anything else is restricted from the highschool. Absolutely nothing would be excluded which

---

[7] *Grundtvigs Skole Verden*, ed. and comp. Knud Eyvin Bugge (Copenhagen, Denmark: G. E. C. Gads Forlag, 1968), II, 97.
[8] Ibid., pp. 202–9.

would be valuable to the students and help to give the institution its special character. He mentions linguistic studies, mathematics, natural history and world history as examples of other subjects. The requirement which he makes for any subject is that it be a "living presentation."

Another characteristic of the highschool was to be the absence of examinations—either entering or leaving. "Our belief in examinations," Grundtvig wrote, "has been shown to be an unfounded superstition." In a humorous sketch which he called "The Sweet Dream," he tells how he dreamed that he returned to Sorø Academy in the twentieth century. There he ran into a student who mistook him for an examination guest. Grundtvig denied this and in the ensuing conversation discovered that it was the custom at the academy to examine the professors: What is more reasonable, asked the student, than that the questions be put to those who claim to know? Grundtvig acknowledged that this was so and could only wonder that things had changed so much from his day.[9]

Though at one point it seemed likely that the King would approve the idea of the academy at Sorø, it was never to be. Grundtvig did see his ideas put into practice at other schools, especially that founded by Kold at Ryslinge (see Chapter 5). A highschool was established by his friends in Zeeland, just north of Copenhagen, which bore Grundtvig's name, and which he visited many times, but he never quite reconciled himself to the fact that there never was a Royal Folk Highschool at Sorø. He died at ninety, having set in motion a movement which has carried his name around the world and earned for him a position as one of Denmark's most illustrious sons.

---

[9] Ibid., pp. 303–5.

3

The School for Life

Grundtvig had envisioned a Norse academy, training citizens for participation in the democratic government. The direction the highschool movement actually took was somewhat different, but in the main his philosophy animated it. The first school which could be called a folk highschool was started at Rødding, in northern Slesvig, in 1844. Christian Flor, a professor of Danish literature at the University of Kiel (which was then on Danish territory), believed that the rising nationalistic spirit of the Germans living in North Slesvig could be countered by using the folk highschool idea to give the peasants, who were Danish, a cultural stronghold. During the war of 1848–58 with Germany, the school's activities were suspended and when the war was won and North Slesvig remained Danish, there were many who felt it should be turned into an agricultural school. Flor, however, believed that its primary task was still to strengthen Danish culture. This question was partially solved when, after the Danish forces were defeated at the hands of the Germans in 1864, Slesvig returned to German rule. At this time the school was moved to its present location at Askov.

The first principal of the school was a young bachelor of divinity named Johan Wegener. Wegener was unprepared for his students' ignorance and lack of refinement and despaired of ever being able to reach them. At Christmas he made up his mind to resign as soon as the winter course was over. But when the students returned from the Christmas vacation, things looked different. In a letter to his fiancee he wrote:

> They pay the most careful attention, they lap up every word, and eagerly make notes about everything. This is better than anything I had thought possible. Their ignorance is abyssmal, but still their spirit is so perceptive that many of them understand the finest shades and the slightest hints.[1]

---

[1] Thomas Rørdam, *The Danish Folk Highschools* (Copenhagen, Denmark: Det Danske Selskab, 1965), p. 48.

In a later letter, Wegener stated that at the time of his leaving both he and the students were in tears.

Flor, himself, replaced Wegener the next year. But while the school, which now had forty-two students, seemed quite success-ful, the inspectors from the Ministry of Education could not un-derstand why the students were not examined daily on their lessons, and why there were no final examinations. In a letter to the ministry, Flor tried to explain that the aim of the school was:

> ... not to force or entice the young to accept a certain kind of in-formation, philosophy, or set of opinions, which we, who are placed on a higher rung of the social ladder, rather than them-selves, wish them to be imbued with. ... The most important re-sult of the teaching of our Highschool is not the actual fund of knowledge and skills, which we try to impart to the students, but rather the mental and spiritual life to which they are awakened. ... All this cannot very well be tested by a public examination.[2]

It need hardly be said that the philosophy expressed in Flor's letter was even more heretical then than it is now. However the authorities did agree to go along with these strange people who were willing to cast their knowledge before the students without requiring anything of those students in return. The question was not settled for good, however, and from time to time there have been attempts on the part of the authorities to disabuse the folk highschool people of their erroneous ways and to require some sort of examinations. The battle even finds its way into the ranks of the highschool people themselves—there seems to be some-thing frightening to many educators about not requiring students to be responsible for factual material which is presented to them.

Flor's successor at Rødding emphasized the importance of enlightened students who had as realistic a picture of life as was possible. Only when they had been able to develop their talents, both of the mind and the spirit, when they had confronted the various views with which they would meet, only then could their mental and spiritual life really become their own property. Thus, at Rødding the pursuit of knowledge was fundamental—enlight-ened, conscientious citizens were the goal. Rødding stands as the

---

2 Ibid., pp. 49–50.

prototype of all the subsequent folk highschools with this academic/spiritual emphasis.

While the initiative for the foundation of Rødding Folk Highschool was taken by university graduates, it was the initiative of the farmer's class itself which resulted in the founding of Uldum Highschool in 1848. The force behind the drive to establish this school was Rasmus Sørensen, a peasant-agitator. Sørensen, the son of a peasant, had graduated from a teachers' seminary and became Uldum's first principal. In his view, the school was to provide for the further education of farm youth who could then represent the common people of the countryside or become, themselves, the leaders and spokesmen of these people.

At Uldum, religious freedom and political rights for the farmers were the goal of the school and its teachers. Thus, a second area of emphasis, though one very much in keeping with Grundtvig's ideas, developed in the highschool movement at its very beginning. At Rødding cultural strength and intellectual growth received the emphasis, along with personal awakening and growth. At Uldum political awareness was added.

A third school was founded in 1850 at Ryslinge. It was established by Christen Kold, a cobbler's son, sometime schoolteacher, missionary's helper and book-binder. As a schoolteacher, Kold's methods got him into trouble with the authorities. He refused to give examinations and to require the children to memorize the lessons. He believed that they learned more and remembered more when motivated by interest than by fear. For this he was relieved of his teaching position. He went to Syria, where he worked as a missionary's helper and book-binder. He had heard of Grundtvig's ideas on education and was greatly impressed by them. When he returned to Denmark he resolved to found a school for the peasants—a folk highschool. He went to Grundtvig to ask for advice and help. From him he received a small sum of money which, together with his own savings, allowed him to rent a small farm with buildings and advertise his school. He sent invitations around the countryside and for the first semester he had fifteen pupils.

Kold had disagreed with Grundtvig over the proper age for such a serious education for boys (for it was only boys who were invited to these first courses. The first coeducational courses were instituted in 1945). Grundtvig, of course, felt that until the youths were eighteen or thereabouts they were not seriously interested in what life was about and had not had enough experience to do any serious questioning. Kold maintained that eighteen was too old— that by that time they were already lost and too interested in their girl and their pipe. Not long after school started, however, Kold found himself coming around to Grundtvig's way of thinking, and found that he had to leave more and more of the teaching of the fifteen year olds to his assistant.

It was Kold's school which established the now traditional five month winter term. Later he introduced a three month summer course for girls. Kold's pedagogy consisted in great part in his talking with the students about the Bible, Bible history, Danish history or thoughts and personalities which had made a great impression on him. Quite often he and the students became so involved that free time and meals were forgotten in the excitement of the discussions. Kold's philosophy of education was simple: first the students must be *enlivened,* then they could be *enlightened.* This is still the pedagogical key to the work at the highschools, no matter what the characteristics or emphases of the individual schools.

Within ten years Kold's school had seventy boys in the winter and fifty girls in the summer. Part of Kold's success must be attributed to the effect of his personality and his teaching methods. Describing them, Ludwig Schrøder, principal at Rødding, wrote:

> It is a sort of Socrates who sits on a chair amid a circle of farm-boys and farm-girls, who have come from afar to visit the School, and all through the day—except when he is lecturing in class—he talks to all these people in such a way that he always evokes their feelings. . . . He lectures for an hour or an hour and a half every morning, when the schoolroom will be full of pupils and guests. Usually he takes as his subject some extract from the World's history, but mainly to apply it to everyday life, a thing he does particularly well. What he wants to awaken is the "heart and spirit.". . .[3]

Especially after he had gotten his larger school, there were always guests attending his lectures. Foremost among these were the

---

[3] Ibid., p. 62.

parents of his students. They had seen how their children had been completely transformed by their stay at the highschool and first came out to see what was going on, then remained out of interest.

Throughout his teaching days, Kold was committed to freedom for his students. He was as committed to it as was Grundtvig. He said:

> The first, the middle, and the last thing I have in mind for my school is liberty, that the children as little as possible, be made to feel that they are walled in by the walls of the school room, and are sitting there to learn, a realization which may in itself be very harmful to the acquisition of knowledge.[4]

Kold's emphasis on the homelike, trustful, and close relations of the school, teachers and pupils, also contributed to the forms which subsequent schools were to take. This atmosphere of trust is essential to the folk highschool way of education. In an atmosphere of trust, free of threat, one is free to learn.

These three pioneer schools established the main trends which were part of the highschool picture in the years to come. More recently other kinds of schools have been founded. Gymnastic highschools were begun to train volunteer leaders in gymnastics and physical training, which are so popular in the Scandinavian countries. In 1910 a workers' school was opened at Esbjerg, the harbor city on the west coast of Jutland. After some indecision about whether it should take a Grundtvigian course or follow the lead of the Swedish Workers' Highschool and become a "free" highschool, the decision was made to take the latter course. This meant that the school would remain non-religious. In their development, the folk highschools in Sweden were not generally linked with any religious movement, while the Danish ones were more or less closely linked with the Grundtvigian religious movement. Later, the *Indre Mission* (Home Missions) movement, a fundamentalist religious movement, established several folk highschools.

Today the Workers Educational Association owns two highschools with an average yearly enrollment of 150 to 200. The students come not only from towns but from the homes of farm

---

[4] Ibid., p. 63.

workers. Somehow two hundred students annually attending the workers' highschools does not sound like much to those of us in the States, where there are more than forty million children in public schools alone. If we remember, though, that Denmark has about the same number of people as Florida, or Indiana, it is easier to put the workers' highschools and the number of their students into perspective. Can we imagine, for example, the workers of Florida or Indiana setting up their own junior college—or whatever institution might be most similar to a folk highschool— and one hundred fifty to two hundred students attending each year, with no diploma or certification in sight? On the same basis, California would have eight to ten workers' highschools, attended by a thousand resident students each year, with several thousand others participating in evening seminars, study circles and the like, the whole partially supported, by way of building loans and student subsidies, by the government. No, we don't see it here in the States, though one can imagine that great changes might ensue from such a program, not to mention the even greater changes which would have to come about before such a program was possible.

At the Danish workers' highschools there is as great a freedom of choice of subjects to be studied as at any "traditional" highschool. They are also experimenting with pedagogical innovations and in addition to the study circle, which was their chief method in the past, they have added "brainstorming," role-playing, "case study" and other techniques.

There are other specialized highschools; nursing highschools, preparatory schools for would-be students of teacher-training seminaries, highschools for child welfare workers, etc. At these preparatory schools some of the courses are acceptable for credits for entry into the seminaries, nursing schools, etc., though they remain folk highschools in every other respect.

One of the most interesting innovations in the folk highschool movement has been the establishment of two schools for the handicapped and disabled. These schools were founded in 1955 and 1956. They especially prepare students for work in public administration or in the technical sector of industry. Many of these students, when they come to the school, are embittered, discouraged, able to see nothing positive in their future. Even if all of them do not leave the school with the prospect of employment, most of them benefit from the experience of several months of fellowship which can give new meaning to their lives. Again, this points up the basic philosophy behind the highschools, that it is concerned with the person first and the vocation second. Or, as Grundtvig himself put it, first the man, then the Christian, emphasizing that whatever we do in life, it is our qualities as a person, as a human being, which determine the qualities of our work.

The question of the encroachment, as some see it, of the vocational into the traditional sphere of the highschool is a vexed one. Obviously, many young people might well consider their time ill-spent on history, art, literature and similar subjects and would like to have something they could get a return on. On the other hand, the tradition of the schools has been to offer a short respite from the daily grind and to present a vista of another side of life —that side which is not governed by the requirements of the daily bread and the roof over the head. Again, there seems to be a growing movement in some quarters for a more practical education for the young, for giving them technical tools with which to make their way in a technological society. This seems to be coupled with a belief that the young people of today are not willing to spend their time at "impractical" pursuits like history, philosophy and art. However, many of the young themselves are opting for just such "impractical" things, even going so far as to set up their own informal schools, and interesting themselves in art, music, nature and self-awareness. There is no denying that the two polar tendencies exist. The difficult question is whether the highschool should be purely "impractical" or, if the practical is to be part of it, how much and for what reasons, and what will be the effect on the traditional goals and role of the school.

If courses which require grades are allowed as part of the curriculum, no matter how small a part, what will be the effect on the traditional relationship of trust and freedom between students and teachers? Will the divisive pressures and the loss of trust which inevitably follow in a situation where grades are required tend to erode the climate for the remaining portion of the highschool's curriculum? On the other hand, will the advantages to the students of learning factual things, practical things, in a folk highschool atmosphere offset the potential disadvantages to the highschool spirit?

The final answers to these questions are not known, and most likely never will be. The debate continues among highschool people, with one positive result being a constant examination of goals and methods which has helped to keep the highschool a viable institution in a time of rapid change.

The question does not concern just the "practicality" of the courses, for the earliest highschools had classes in arithmetic, bookkeeping, language, and farm management. The real problem lies not in whether or not courses are practical, but in the use of such courses as prerequisites for other courses or as qualifying courses for other institutions. For this requires some sort of grading system, some way of evaluating how well a student has done, how well prepared he is, how much he knows. Immediately, we have two undesirable side effects. The first is the loss of communication and trust between teacher and student in an evaluative atmosphere; the second is a subtle tendency in any such situation to push for the students acquiring that knowledge, achieving that level of competence, which is necessary for recommendation.

And, to be honest, how else could it be? If the school is to have, as part of its *raison d'etre*, the preparation and recommendation of students for some other institution, it is in its best interest that those recommendations are respected. It is highly likely that if it recommended all students indiscriminately, the value of its recommendations would decline in the eyes of the recipient institution—and no doubt also in the eyes of most of the students. So as soon as the highschool undertakes to become, in effect, a training school—a preparatory school—it is faced with the necessity of evaluating, grading, and sorting the students. And with this comes a potential breakdown of one of the essential things a highschool has to offer—an open, non-evaluative learning situation.

This problem did not exist in the early days of the highschools, even though they offered "practical" subjects. For in the end, it was the students themselves who evaluated what they got from the highschool experience. The school did not guarantee to them or their parents to bring them to a certain competency in arithmetic or language or dairy keeping. It was this very refusal to offer recommendations or diplomas which enabled the highschool to be what it is and to develop its particular genius.

It is true that over the years experience has seemed to show that young people who have been at a highschool do often become better, more progressive farmers, more successful dairymen, clerks and nurses who give better, more human service, and so on. There are nursing schools now, for instance, which give preference to students who have been to a highschool—with nothing said about courses or grades, the highschool experience itself being the important factor. Hospitals have found that former highschool students seem to have a more human, caring attitude toward the patients.

A large department store in Copenhagen partially subsidizes highschool courses for its salespeople. The management believes that the warmer, more human response to customers by those who have been to a highschool more than repays the cost. Yet, again, the highschools don't give courses in salesmanship, or nursing, or how to treat customers.

The question of vocationalism has not been settled philosophically and perhaps never will be. On the practical level, however, a working solution to the question of just how much vocational training a school can have and still qualify as a folk highschool came in a Ministry of Education order in 1943. This order requires that at least half the lessons and a minimum of twenty-four periods per week must be devoted to non-vocational subjects.

Why is it important for the Ministry to know when a school is a folk highschool and when it is not? At first glance it might seem quite unimportant. However, the facts of life apply even to such a spiritual undertaking as a folk highschool. The facts in this case are that the Danish government provides support, through the Folk Highschool and Agricultural School Law, for both the schools and their students. Since this support, both direct and indirect, reaches as high as seventy percent of the school's running expenses, it can be very important whether or not a school is recognized as a folk highschool.

State subsidies have been a part of the highschool picture since the very beginning. In 1852, only two years after the start of the school at Ryslinge, the grant was about a thousand dollars. Through the efforts of the Friends of the Farmers in parliament, it had risen to about three thousand dollars in 1857. In return for these subsidies, however, the government demanded the introduction of examinations. The highschool people and their supporters fought this requirement. The government eventually withdrew its demand for examinations, but in the 1870's an inspector was appointed to visit the schools and see for himself how they were working. The first inspector was sympathetic to the schools and the system has worked well. The inspector is not an inspector in the usual sense of finding possible faults or making rules for the teaching. His duty is to get to know the schools, their principals and staffs, to make sure their syllabi are those of folk highschools, and that they do not aim primarily at vocational training. In practice this inspector, who is now the government director of all education for young adults in Denmark, has usually been chosen from highschool circles. The present director, for example, was formerly a principal of Askov Highschool.

Government support grew through the years until in 1942, in a move to make possible the attendance of more children of town workers and small holders and farm laborers, a Highschool Act increased the government grants both to the impecunious students and the schools themselves.

The act, known as the Act of 1942, has three sections: Scholarships for Students; Grants for Expenses of the Schools; and Loans for Buildings, etc. The average student support level is fifty percent of the students' expenses. In the case of needy students the level rises to ninety percent or above and in certain cases exservicemen may receive one hundred percent support. The support is proportional to the parents' income and capital. Today about seventy-seven percent of the male students and seventy-two percent of the female receive some support from the government.

In discussing the government support of the highschools and their students, it is important to deal with a possible misapprehension which might arise. This is the question of whether this assistance, in fact, distorts the picture of the actual student interest in the schools. "Of course they come to the folk schools," one might say, "all their expenses are paid. But would they still come if there was no government assistance?" While we must remember that the average assistance amounts to only fifty percent of the student's expenses, the answer to that question is obviously "No, there wouldn't be as many students in that case," just as there wouldn't be as many college students in this country if they all had to pay high tuition expenses. It is in this respect that I think the question—which at first seems to be a reasonable one—is misleading. For the educational level of a country is not judged by the opportunities available to the small number of people who can afford an expensive education, but by the extent to which the opportunity for a quality education is offered to each citizen, regardless of his economic situation or his ability to pay. In a democracy, therefore, the question might preferably be: "Does this government subvention enable students to attend the folk highschools and benefit from them who would otherwise be unable to?" This is indeed what happens; it is, in fact, the rationale behind the government program of aid to non-public education. So, though it may at first seem that the success of the highschools may be due in part to the government subventions, this is no more true of the highschools than it is of the public schools and universities. How many children would be in school if the state did not provide the education free in the interests of the society as a whole? I believe that those students who attend highschools because of the money are rather few, and that by and large most who go do so because they want to.

It is important in any discussion of the financial aspects of education in Denmark to remember that while the average Dane enjoys a freedom from many worries because of the extent of the social welfare program, he has much less surplus money at his disposal than his American counterpart. The average Dane does not have a car. Two or three car families are almost unknown there. Refrigerators, automatic washers and dryers are still rare. Few people own houses with any surrounding ground. It is just not as easy for a Danish citizen to come up with enough money to send someone off to school.

The question of money becomes even more critical considering the kind of experience which is offered by the folk highschool. It is not one which can be amortized over the ensuing years, as a consequence of getting a better job, for example. The value of the highschool experience, as we have said, lies entirely within the life of the person. It is not easy to place a monetary value upon it. If it has an economic dimension, it can only be the tenuous one of the individual having become "enlivened" by his highschool experience and going out and doing a better job at what he turns his hand to. This did seem to happen to the farm youth in the early days of the highschool, when former highschool students became the leaders of the enlightened and progressive farmers who started cooperatives and initiated the changeover from grain growing to meat raising when the bottom fell out of the grain market in the 1880's. It can happen today—we remember the preference of some nursing schools for those with a highschool background, and the practice of the large Copenhagen department store of subsidizing a highschool stay for its young clerks. But this is a side effect, and cannot be considered in the same light as the technician's training or that of the computer programmer or engineer. The rewards of the folk highschool experience are intangibles: an increased contact with and awareness of the richness of the world, of the rewards of working with and interacting with one's fellows, and the experience of the adventure of learning.

Grants for the expenses of the schools themselves can be broken down into: (a) a small basic grant of less than five hundred dollars, plus three and one-half percent of the value of the buildings, furniture and accessories, or up to fifty percent of the rent if the school is housed in rented premises; (b) seventy percent of the salaries for teachers and principal, direct increments for the salaries of staff who have served for a certain number of years; and (c) fifty percent of the expenses for educational materials.

The loans for buildings can be for up to fifty percent of the value of the school in question or, if improvements to existing schools, up to seventy-five percent of the value of the improvements. In all cases no payments are required, but interest must be paid at the rate of four percent per annum.[5]

Thus, the government has a commitment to the folk highschool. This government support of independent, unregulated private schools is unfamiliar to us and, indeed, is evidence of a quite

---

[5] Harald Engberg-Pedersen, *Hojskolestatistik 1954/55–1964/65*, Danish Ministry of Education Bulletin (Copenhagen, Denmark, 1966), pp. 1–3.

different philosophy of education which exists in the Scandinavian countries. There, if a school is serving an educational function, it is deemed to deserve support from the government. According to the Danish constitution, parents are not compelled to send their children to a public elementary school, but only bound to see that their children get an education not inferior to that provided by the public elementary school. An enlightened and concerned citizenry is the goal in all three of the Scandinavian countries and this takes precedence over the smaller questions of who gets to educate whom.

4

The Folk Highschool as Experience

There is a quality we sometimes experience on a warm spring day, when we want to greet each passerby and the whole world seems to be our friend. Sometimes we experience it instead on hearing a particular piece of music. It is a moment when we feel lighter, when tiredness does not exist, when joy and excitement suffuse everything. It has been experienced by mountain climbers, by artists, by people in sensitivity groups, and even—rarely—by students in school. Sometimes, when a class has coalesced around a discussion of some subject and student and teacher become inextricably bound up together and share that moment in time, simultaneously on an emotional and intellectual level, it *is* experienced by students. It is like the feeling which prompts us to exclaim when a discussion has moved to the coffee shop or grass, "I've learned more in this discussion than in the whole semester of classes; why isn't school like this?"

We can call this feeling being "turned on," a feeling of being closely in touch with, and involved in, one's fellows, one's activities, and all of life. Some people are this way all the time; but they are a lucky few. Others achieve the state occasionally, some rarely or never. One of the things which happens at a folk highschool is that people become "turned on." Grundtvig and Kold called it "enlivenment." Whatever it is called, it is an essential part of the highschool experience. It is an essential part of any meaningful educational experience.

I was "enlivened" during my visits to representative highschools. The students with whom I came into contact were, in most cases, also "enlivened"; so were the teachers. For many, the experience at a folk highschool is akin to what Maslow calls a "peak experience"—a time when one seems to be fully alive and in tune with all about him.

My official study of the folk highschool began at the Graduate School for Foreign Students at the University of Copenhagen, though I had read several books about them before making the decision to study in Denmark. At the University I spent five months studying the Danish language and Danish history and economics at the graduate school. At the same time, under the direction of my advisor, the late Johannes Novrup, I studied Grundtvig's life and the folk highschool movement.

I was not scheduled to visit any of the schools until the following spring—by which time my background would better enable me to evaluate the experience and my Danish would permit me to take part. As the date for my departure from Copenhagen drew near, however, my enthusiasm waned. I was not at all anxious to go. I did not want to leave the stimulation of the university life in the capital for what looked to be a very dull and "uplifting" time among the farmers.

It was strange that though I believed in what the highschools were doing, they hadn't impressed me as something particularly exciting or enjoyable. It was somewhat of a shock to realize the extent to which I had accepted the stereotype of "schools for farmers" which has stuck to the highschools through the years. This stereotype has some basis in fact, of course. A large part of the movement's history is tied up with the farmers and their cause, and even today the percentage of rural youth attending the schools is higher than for those from the cities. Yet, I should have learned from my studies that what the highschools offered was neither exclusively for farm youth nor even primarily for them; that what was offered was of equal value to all, irrespective of background or place of residence, even of age. Instead, I reacted at least partially in terms of the stereotyped picture held by those who know a little about the folk highschools but have not experienced them for themselves, nor had close acquaintances who did.

I believe a part of the explanation for my attitude must lie in the method by which I learned about the schools. Instead of visiting the schools immediately, or talking to students who had just come away from a highschool stay, I went to books. In fact, I read Grundtvig's words "dead are letters, even if they be written with the fingers of angels, and dead is all knowledge which does not find response in the life of the reader," without realizing that they also applied to my situation. For reading about the folk highschools did not prepare me for the actual experience. The words left so much out that was important in the real experience that

mere studying about them—no matter how assiduously—failed to
provide the whole story. I was also to discover later, when I began
to write about the highschools, the truth of the second part of that
statement, concerning response in the life of the reader. I found
that, with the educational experiences we have had in the public
schools, we are unable to put ourselves into the kind of an educational situation which the folk highschool is. How many of us have
experienced an educational situation which has been both good
for us and exciting, so that we could conjure up an image of what
one would be like in the living flesh? Actually, there are a lot more
people today who have had just such experiences than there were
back in the fifties, which is one of the reasons a book such as this is
possible now. There are exciting things going on in education and
they have whetted peoples' appetites. The idea of a school without grades or diplomas does not sound nearly so impossible today,
in this day of free schools and free universities.

I think that another reason for some of the misunderstandings
of the highschools, though, lies with the historians of the movement. It is as though, in wanting to build a strong case for the importance of the highschools, in pointing out the accomplishments
which were most impressive and which couldn't be denied, they
left out something else. That something else we might characterize
as the universal message or the universal validity of the highschools
for young people of all backgrounds. When this element was left
out, what was left looked very much like a school for farmers. It is
easy to understand why this is so. The early accomplishments of
the highschools, the most profound effects, the most measurable
effects, had to do with the farmers. The cooperative movement,
which has been crucially important to the very viability of Denmark's economic position in the world, has been almost wholly a
rural phenomenon. While there are a few consumers' cooperatives
operating in the cities, the great majority of them, growers and
producers coops, buyers' coops, are connected with farmers and
dairymen. The cooperative movement came into being largely
through the efforts of highschool people who had learned the
value of trust and cooperation in their living together at the
schools. In the area of legislation, many former highschool teachers and students have been in government and, while observers
often credit the folk highschool movement for much of the pro-

gressive legislation in Denmark, it is again in the area of legislation relating to agriculture that the influence can be most clearly traced.

While the chroniclers presented a factual picture of the high-school and did not, in fact, leave out the rest of the picture, what emerged was unmistakably a school for farmers, a place where, from the special viewpoint of urban young people, you could go for an uplifting time among clean-scrubbed, serious kids from the country. If this was not your idea of an educationally or socially exciting way to spend a winter, singing psalms and hearing about Grundtvig—well, the folk highschool wasn't for you. And, to tell the truth, on the face of it a winter at a highschool doesn't sound as interesting or exciting as a winter in the city, especially when one's friends are in the city and not at the highschool. That is exactly the feeling I had, in fact, when it came time for me to leave my friends in the city to spend part of the winter at a highschool.

It may be that to young people living in the country, more removed from their friends by distance, with fewer movies and dances to attend, a winter at a highschool did not appear as a dull prospect at all. It might also be argued that the rural youth *were* more clean-scrubbed and serious. But, at least with respect to knowing what to expect from the highschool experience, they have had an advantage over their contemporaries in the cities. They have had friends or relatives who had been to a highschool and who could tell them, in terms of personal experience, what it was like. It has been estimated that as many as one in three of the rural population in Denmark has attended a highschool at one time. At this rate, it would be few young people in the country who did not know someone who had attended. If there was anything positive to be gotten from the experience, it would be these friends and relatives who would best be able to communicate it. The statistics seem to bear this out. Among the reasons given by students for attending highschools, the largest percentage mention having learned of it through a friend or relative, often a parent.

My own situation was not unlike that of the urban youth. I had graduated from college, had spent two years in the navy, had knocked around the world a bit, and was somewhat older than the average highschool student. I enjoyed the life in Copenhagen, the dances, the social contact with my friends among the university students. Life at a folk highschool did not look inviting in comparison. Still, I went through with my plans and traveled around to a number of highschools. As I went from school to school, sharing in the life and talking to students and teachers, I found my attitude toward the schools changing. I began to be caught up in the excitement of the learning process the young people were going through, and the strong feeling of community which existed at the schools. I began to catch a glimpse of what it was that had kept young people coming to these schools for the more than a century they have been in existence. I also began to see what a learning community really was, and how far from it most of our educational experiences were.

For there was an excitement among these young people I encountered at the highschools, an excitement which resulted partly from the attitudes they brought with them—for they had, after all, chosen to come to these schools which didn't give diplomas or certificates of competence—but which also was due partly to the life at the school itself. It was a life which might be characterized, I suppose, as a community on a joint venture into the world of learning. Students, teachers, all were in the thing together. There wasn't the usual barrier between students and teachers which we find in our ordinary schools—a barrier enforced by grades, required courses, separation of teachers and students (initiated by the teachers, themselves, in most cases, I realize), and the position of the teacher as the official dispenser of the codified knowledge of the society. At the folk highschool these barriers do not exist—or, more probably, they exist, but to a significantly lesser degree. The philosophy of the schools opposes them, and the very forms within which the schools operate discourage them. Teachers, for example, take their meals in the dining room with the students. They do not sit at a separate "faculty" table, but at the same tables as the students. If the teacher wishes an intellectual discussion with his lunch, it is in his own interest to awaken the students to the joys of such discussions, for it will be with them such discussions will have to take place.

The teachers' contracts also usually state that they must make one night a week available to students who want to visit them. It really is quite impossible for a teacher at a highschool to retreat. Thus, the very structure of the school opens up the possibility of student-teacher interaction. The principal, himself, is not exempt from this openness. He cannot lock himself away in his office to do paperwork (or whatever it is that principals do). In all Danish public schools, including the largest, the principal carries a teaching load, usually of several hours a day. This practice is also followed at the folk highschools. Besides this, the principal of a folk highschool is to a much greater degree than in the public schools the real shaper behind the spirit of the individual school. As a consequence, he feels a need to take part in the educational process of his school. He usually takes the responsibility for one of the daily lectures which the entire student body of the school is expected to attend, besides teaching one or more classes. And he, too, eats in the common dining room with the teachers and students.

Besides these ways of encouraging interaction between students and teachers, there is the matter of the teachers, themselves. They just do not go to a folk highschool to teach unless they are willing to commit themselves to the openness that exists. The pay is less than that at a public school, the hours, as in any boarding school, are longer, the demands for relevance of subject matter are much greater. When you have only your subject and the way you present it to capture and retain the students' interest, it is much more important that what you say has some relevance for them, some significance. There are no grades, no future examinations to be held over their heads to make them pay attention. It can be a very threatening situation, of course. As a consequence, in general only teachers who are quite dedicated to the idea of free learning are attracted to the highschool milieu. As the current Director of Education for Folk Highschools and Agricultural Schools explained it: "If the truth be known, one should preferably be a little of a pedagogical enthusiast in order to be a highschool teacher." Teachers at a highschool are typically there because they feel that in their lives there has been something which they value highly. They want to share this something with the students. The highschool teacher seeks to involve the student; this means he must himself be involved.

One of the most surprising results of my stay at the various highschools became evident when I returned to Copenhagen at the end of my tour to write a paper on my experiences. I had regretfully left my friends and the excitement of the capital, fully expecting to be bored. When I returned, and began to take up again where I had left off I was shocked to discover that in the short period of my absence my friends and their social gatherings had become boring. The experience was a strange one and I wondered about it. It seemed that the "enlivened" young people I had met on my tour made the university students I knew seem narrow and shallow by comparison. The stimulation which was always present in the folk highschool environment was lacking in the university environment. The students at the university seemed to me not nearly so involved with life and with the great questions of life, they did not seem to be always going out to meet life, as was the case with so many of the young people I had met at the highschool. There had been something about those young people who were enthusiastic and questioning and eager to participate in the world, even though they may have had quite limited intellectual experience or had never been outside the small town they were born in, which captured one much more than the erudition and sophistication of the university students.

As I turned my surprising experience over in my mind I saw what I felt to be clear distinctions between the experience of the highschool students and the university students which helped account for the difference in my reactions to them. At the university all the students were studying "subjects." That is, they were learning facts about things. They were doing this in a situation where there was a master and an acolyte; the professor was the master (or it might be the books), and they were the acolytes, depending upon the good will and approbation of the master for their future. Even before this, though, they had to have spent a number of years in similar circumstances, at the gymnasium. Only a select group of students goes to the gymnasium from the middle school. Entrance to the gymnasium is based almost wholly on grades earned before the age of eleven. To gain entrance to the university from the gymnasium, students must take a national test, which only a small percentage pass. If they pass, tuition at the university is free. But, to have finally made it to the university means that a student has concerned himself mainly with facts for at least six years of his life. His whole orientation has largely been aimed toward books and impressing the professor. There has been little time for going out to meet life or for examining his own place in life—his meaning, his place in the scheme of things. This is not to say that the Danish university student is not outgoing, fun-loving, psychologically healthy, or physically active. On the contrary he, like all his European confreres, seems to be very active. But examination of life goals, or serious questioning of what life might really be all about—there has not been time for that. Besides, of course, if you begin questioning your goals you may end up abandoning them. That is a dangerous thing to do at a university.

At the highschools, in contrast to the fact-dominated, future-oriented existence, there was an emphasis on the present concerns of the student, on the world as he experienced it and would experience it when he went back to his home. Grundtvig wrote: "First the man, then the Christian." He was aware that it is always the person who makes the role important or negligible, large or small, beneficial or destructive. At the highschool, therefore, it is people, living in a day-to-day world, who are important. And it is only through the people, in a manner of speaking, that the subject matter—the philosophy, sociology, psychology, history, etc.—becomes living and valuable. It is only as it affects the life of an individual person that any fact, any theory, takes on meaning and importance. "Dead is all knowledge," wrote Grundtvig, "which does not find response in the life of the reader."

This spirit, which I attribute to the highschools—rather, which I felt in the students—was not universal. I did not feel it equally strongly at all schools or from all students. However, this is only to be expected. Some of the students were more enlivened by the experience, some less. At some schools there was less a feeling of joyous commitment to life and more of a serious approach to it. At some schools I felt warmly drawn into the life of the school; at others I felt left outside and was rather glad to leave. Again, this is certainly to be expected. My own personality would cause me to respond more quickly and warmly to some environments than to others. With each school strongly influenced by the personality of its principal, so that each has, in effect, its own personality, it is inevitable that this would occur. One thing I was very interested to discover, however, was that at schools where I was obliged to share a room with one of the students, I found the reception warmer and was made to feel a member of the community in a much shorter time. Where I had a room to myself, I pretty much remained a visitor, an outsider, and missed much of what was going on. There was something about having someone to take you around with him, something about being known as so-and-so's roommate, which helped to open up friendships. At the schools where I had a roommate I attended parties, discussions, excursions which I could never have known about had I been on my own. It seems to me this is another example of the wisdom of the founders of the highschool when they emphasized the communal life and specified that the school should be a boarding school. Sharing a room can be a trying experience. But it also can be a key to experiences and friendships which would otherwise be unavailable.

I began my tour of the highschools at the International Folk Highschool at Elsinore, which is also known as The International Peoples College. Because many of its students come from other lands, it has been found to be more politic to call the school a college than to refer to it as a highschool, though it follows the Grundtvigian traditions. International Peoples College was chosen because from its beginning it has concentrated on providing a folk highschool experience for students from outside of Denmark. While many of its students do come from Denmark, a typical semester is likely to find Americans, Britons, Germans, French, Japanese, Africans, or Indians. There are often groups attending from eastern European countries, and South America, also. Instruction at the school generally takes place in Danish, English and German, though other languages may be used, depending upon the abilities of the teachers and the needs of the students.

It was at this school that I got my first inkling of that part of the folk highschool which did not come through in the books. I found that an essential part of the life at a highschool was discussions. They took place at all hours; in the morning between classes, at the noon break, before dinner, during the evening. They were held in the students' rooms, in the hallways, in the parlor. Each person brought with him a cup and a spoon, and a can of Nescafé and some hot water would make the rounds. These Nescafé-klatches were ubiquitous and lively. Their subject was life. We talked about religion, the race problem, philosophy, the future, sex, psychology, politics—any subject dealing with life. We asked each other what it was like to live in the various countries we had come from—Japan, England, Germany, the U.S., India, Australia, Denmark—and what we would do when we returned home.

This same interest in discussion stands in my mind as one of the central features of the concept of the folk highschool. It was the presence or absence of these informal discussions—my participation in them, my being drawn into them—which had a lot to do with how I felt about a school, how much of the life I was able to enter into, and the amount of excitement I felt. At schools where there either was little of this informal discussion or where I was not drawn into what there was, I felt little of the warmth I felt at other schools where I found myself taking part.

It is difficult to reconstruct the content, but in such situations it is not the subjects that are important as such, so much as the effect on the participants. I suppose if it could be described it would be something to the effect that the real subject of the discussions was people, the importance of caring, and one's commitment to mankind in general. The young people were usually open, unguarded. They were ready to talk about themselves, their hopes and their experiences. Because of this openness, it was quite easy to strike up acquaintances; people spoke when they passed one another, even though they might not be personally acquainted. This was true to some degree at all the schools I visited. A camaraderie existed which made communication easier, and made establishing contact with another individual easier. This is not to say that everything at a highschool is rosy or that all the students are self-actualized. At Askov, for example, there was a tendency for students to form into cliques. Both students and teachers were aware of this problem and the fact that it tended to work against the community feeling in the school, and when I was there they were trying to find a solution, but without too much success.

In general, though, and considering the wide differences between highschools—with some very conservative and staid and others very radical and concerned intimately with social problems —this camaraderie, this feeling of being a member of a community with the freedom of communication which goes along with it, characterizes the folk highschools and is one of their unique offerings.

5

The New Humanism

"In every hour the human race begins," writes Martin Buber. Despite the fact that each child is born with a share of the world-history, into a given situation of "world-historical" significance, in this hour, as in every hour:

> ... what has not been invades the structure of what is, with ten thousand countenances, of which not one has been seen before, with ten thousand souls still undeveloped but ready to develop—a creative event if ever there was one ... primal potential might. This potentiality, streaming unconquered, however much of it is squandered, is the reality *child*.
>
> What greater care could we cherish or discuss than that this grace may not henceforth be squandered as before, that the might of newness may be preserved for renewal? Future history is not inscribed by the pen of a causal law on a roll which merely awaits unrolling; its characters are stamped by the unforeseeable decisions of future generations.[1]

Certainly a poetic vision of the value of education: whatever value education can claim lies in its relationship to children. And, in the widest sense, we could include as children all of humanity, for mankind is much like a child, continually seeking to learn— more about himself, more about the universe, and the overriding question of all: the meaning of life. As an individual, too, man spends his life learning.

Taken even in the narrowest sense, Buber's "child" includes any young person, since young people through their school years, and often beyond, are cast in the role of "child." This enforced role-designation, in fact, has tended to reduce the concept of "child" to a pejorative one. No one wants to be considered a child. Young people in school, especially today, resent the role they are forced into—that of the passive child vis-a-vis the dominant, par-

---

[1] Martin Buber, *Between Man and Man* (London, England: Routledge and Kegan Paul, 1947), pp. 83–4.

ent-figure teacher. Buber's idea of "child" rejects this view. His "child" is an entity, a Being with integrity and infinite value, with a contribution to make to history. Now it becomes the privilege of society—and the school—to assist in the growth of this child, this new beginning of the human race.

In the thought-provoking book *Inventing Education for the Future*,[2] Robert Bickner points up a crucial consequence of the pejorative idea of child with respect to education: "One of the ironies of our society is that our schools are often viewed as successful institutions, while our children are often viewed as disappointments." (p. 55) Once we become aware of this irony we see other strange manifestations of our approach to education. As an example, take the pass and fail concept of grades. Just who is it that is passing or failing? It seems a most grievous misunderstanding of both human beings and institutions to assume that the school succeeds and child fails. If the schools exist to educate the child and the child is not educated, who failed? If education is *for* the child, rather than the other way around, it must be the school that has failed. The mechanic we have paid to repair our car, the painter we have paid to paint our house, would be laughed at if they explained their failure to do their job by saying "It is the fault of your car" or "It is the fault of your house—it just won't be painted." Yet we unquestioningly sign our child's report cards which report that the child is failing to become educated, or is only being half educated—that he just won't accept education. The report cards implicitly blame the child and by indirection ourselves, since it is well-known that not only do our children receive their intellectual abilities from their genes, but that children from disadvantaged homes do less well in school than those from advantaged ones. If our children don't do well we are obviously to blame. At the same time they reject any notion of failure on the part of the school. Education, in fact, seems no longer something which we do for the child, but rather something which the child does for the school, somewhat as if the mechanic charges us for the extent to which he is unable to repair our car, rather than the extent to which he *is* able to repair it. Does it not seem strange that when a child does not do well in school we are

---

[2] Robert Bickner, "After the Future, What?" in *Inventing Education for the Future*, ed. Werner Z. Hirsch (San Francisco: Chandler Publishing Company, 1967).

disappointed in *him?* What is the great power we suppose this child to have that we expect from him infallibility in his dealings with institutionalized education?

Buber's "child," however, cannot be failed by the educational system, for the system derives its only meaning from its ability to serve the child, to cherish it. This is the approach to education which the "new humanist" takes.

But what is the new humanism in practical terms? Who speaks for it? Who are its gods and prophets? What are its heaven, its hell? In the new humanism what is Man?

What I call the new humanism is not really new. It has its roots in the far past. There have been many who have seen man with what might be called "new humanistic" eyes. Grundtvig, a Lutheran bishop, was one. In China, about the year 201 B.C., Mencius wrote the following:

> The Bull Mountain was once covered with lovely trees. But it is near the capital of a great state. People came with their axes and choppers; they cut the woods down, and the mountain has lost its beauty. Yet, even so, the day air and the night air came to it, rain and dew moistened it. Here and there fresh sprouts began to grow. But soon cattle and sheep came along and browsed on them, and in the end the mountain became gaunt and bare, as it is now. And seeing it thus gaunt and bare, people imagine that it was woodless from the start. Now just as the natural state of the mountain was quite different from what now appears, so too, in every man (little though they may be apparent) there assuredly were once feelings of decency and kindness; and if these good feelings are no longer there, it is that they have been tampered with, hewn down with axe and bill. As each day dawns they are assailed anew. What chance then has our nature, any more than the mountain, of keeping its beauty? . . . so that any one might make the same mistake about us as about the mountain, and think that there was never any good in us from the very start. Yet assuredly our present state of feeling is not what we began with. Truly,
> > "If rightly tended, no creature but thrives;
> > If left untended, no creature but pines away" [3]

What is important in Mencius' statement is not the idea of man's fall, but the idea that he is originally and essentially "good," and that the good struggles for existence until completely over-

---

[3] Arthur Waley, *The Way and Its Power: A Study of the Tao Te Ching and Its Place in Chinese Thought* (New York: Grove Press, 1958), pp. 18–19. Printed with permission of George Allen and Unwin, Ltd.

come by adversity. For creatures to thrive, they, no less than the plants, must have a supportive environment. The idea that man is essentially "good" or positive, or even beautiful by nature, essentially, from the inside, is crucial to the position of the new humanism. This does not mean that his goodness will prevail regardless of circumstances, because this obviously is not so. This goodness (certainly not the best word to describe man's nature, but what other do we have?) is, as it were, instinctoid, a part of our natures, but unlike the instincts of the animals, is relatively weak and fragile—easily repressed or killed. There are some of the new humanists who believe that man would be better described as inherently possessing a potential for good *or* evil, that he is neutral but can move in either direction, depending on the situation which exerts its force on him. This may well be the case, though it calls to mind the question: Can destructive societies produce constructive men, and how? The appearance of such people, for they do appear, has usually been ascribed to faulty socialization—to their somehow not having responded properly to the socialization process. Is it possible that what happened instead was a true resistance to the socialization process? Perhaps we'll never know, yet there are many today—often not among the recognized authorities—who, having seen gentle, loving, positive persons emerge when hostile, destructive people were allowed to discard several layers of their socialization, believe that such may indeed be the truth of the matter.

"Humanism will not change human nature," writes the humanist Hamilton Fyfe.[4]

> Human nature does not need to be changed. What Humanism does is to encourage and emphasize its kindly, rational elements so that these may prevail against the harshness and cruelty, the selfishness and greed which have tended to overlay them, this tendency being a result of perverted civilization.

Though others through the years have spoken of this view of man, we may be more familiar with contemporary explanations of this philosophy which I call the new humanism. The names of Martin Buber, Carl Rogers, Hubert Bonner, George Herbert

---

[4] H. Fyfe, "Humanism as a World-Unifying Force" *The Humanist* 1 (1953), 15.

Mead, William James, John Dewey, Abraham Maslow, Arthur Combs, and Sidney Jourard stand in the front rank of a band whose number increases steadily, and they by no means begin to exhaust the list. In fact, to extend the list would still result in leaving out as many important speakers for man as one included. This has not always been the case. Not so long ago, there were a few lone voices speaking in behalf of man as a self-actualizing, positively oriented creature.

During the past twenty years, however, a new force has appeared on the scene in psychology, especially American psychology. Called variously the Third Force (to distinguish it from the two earlier "forces," psychoanalysis and behaviorism), being psychology, humanistic psychology, it has brought to us a new way of looking at man. Psychologists involved in this movement are associated with many emphases. In the group may be found personalists, humanists, self-psychologists, phenomenologists, transactionists, and existentialists. All have in common a deep concern with questions of man's being and becoming. They take a view of behavior that is highly consistent with the experience of superior teachers: It is a point of view that sees people as growing, dynamic organisms. It regards human beings not as things to be made or molded, but as unique entities in the process of becoming.

One of the key points in this view of man is the primacy of a need for adequacy, for self-actualization, for the person to believe that he is worth something as a human being. This need is the fundamental motivation of the human being throughout his life. It governs his relationships with others, his constant attempts to learn the things which will enable him to cope with and control his environment. This drive is not learned. It is present in the infant who seeks to make sense of his environment and practices skills constantly. It is in the adult who, knowing that he is not functioning properly on the psychic level, seeks a therapist. And it is the same drive which, as the therapist helps to remove the blocks that lie in the path of recovery, directs the person toward healthy growth. But this drive, tenacious though it is, is weak in contrast to the enormous pressures which society brings to bear on the organism. It is difficult to resist these pressures; for most it is impossible. It is made doubly difficult by the fact that the only definition we have had of what a person is came from the very society which exerted these pressures. The only opposition was that which came from that weak voice within saying "They mustn't do this to me. . . . I have to be true to myself, not to them" or some such words. Such attempts to resist the process of molding have not been greeted with glad cries from the educational institutions. We have always tended to regard those children who resisted our shaping efforts as somehow irrelevant, damaged, dangerous. Today many of us are beginning to see many of these resisters as being more relevant, less damaged, less dangerous to themselves and the human race than the others whom we have successfully carried along. For as we look more and more critically at the methods of our educational establishment, and even at the goals, and especially at the results, to many of us it appears that many of the children who resisted us so firmly were, in fact, preserving their own integrity, their own uniqueness, their own humanity, which the system was seeking to submerge and replace with uniformity and acquiescence.

The importance of this inner motivation, this inner drive of the organization to maintain its integrity, is one of the building blocks on which the new humanism is built. It is this drive which, as much as anything else, distinguishes man as he is seen by the new humanists. It is this drive which is manifested in the organism's self-actualizing tendencies, its continuing drive toward adequacy. This drive brings us to another of the characteristics of man as seen by the new humanism. In order to pursue the goal of self-actualization, in order to become adequate, man must possess the power of choice. We cannot benefit from our experience if we are not free to make decisions—decisions which may be either right or wrong. Therefore, for the new humanism, man must be free. Otherwise he cannot be responsible. There is no need here to go into the hoary argument about whether or not man *is* free. Suffice it to say that it is an essential part of the philosophy of the new humanism that at least in substantial part, man be free, that he be a maker of decisions that matter; that, in fact, he is a maker of his own goals and values, and until evidence is forthcoming that man is determined, that there is no free will, we may regard him as free. For, if man is not free, able to make decisions unique to himself, it is ridiculous to hold him responsible for his actions. The only evidence which could demonstrate beyond a doubt that man is determined is that evidence which is required in any discipline

—predictability. Until it is possible to predict accurately the future, we may feel free to assume that there is an area of freedom in which man's actions are meaningful. In this case, metaphysical exhortation will not suffice for proof.

Another feature of man in the new humanist view is his social nature. Man's nature is not to be found in isolated individuals, any more than it is to be found in isolated parts of any one individual. A human being's bonds with his generation and his society are his essence; in order to know what man is, therefore, we must study him in his relationships—in real life. Though each person is unique, though he brings into this world a unique combination of qualities, it is in his social interaction that he grows and learns and becomes what he is potentially. All that happens to him involves contact with his society, from his learning to smile by watching his mother smile at him to his learning about his environment through a language which is unique to his society. Man can become whole not by himself, but in relation to another, or to others.

Perhaps the final major facet of the new humanism is the recognition of the vital role which the emotions play in being human. Our traditional view seems to have been that the emotions were somehow of a lower order than the intellect, that they were a handicap, a less than human throwback to our animal ancestors (if we believe in evolution), or a throwback to our original expulsion from the garden of Eden (if we reject evolution as an explanation of man's past). It has always been one of the goals of self-improvement, whether in a Saint Matthew or Paul or a physical scientist of today, to develop rational control over the emotions, to be realistic, unemotional, to free oneself from the thrall of this undesirable and untrustworthy side of ourselves. Things that appeal to the emotions have always occupied a lower level in our hierarchy of values. "Don't be emotional" is the insult supreme in an argument. The emotions, emotional behavior, have always been assigned to those less evolved creatures, the women. (Alas for male superiority, this cannot be done in the world of the new humanism.) The behavioral scientist, in attempting to chart the inner workings of man, has had as his *bête noir* man's irrational, emotional tendencies, which render meaningless many precise, beautifully designed experiments, and it has been his constant goal to isolate and eliminate them.

In the new humanism, however, the emotions are recognized

as part of the person, as much a part as his intellect or his digestive system or his muscles. They have as great a role to play as any of these and to attempt to live, or act, without being influenced by them is just as impossible. They are a part of what it is to be alive. At the same time, it has become clear that the emotions are not some force which is in conflict with the intellect, as we have so long been led to believe. They are not two, contrary forces battling for control of man's nature, but are two complementary aspects of the one nature. They can no more be separated than you can separate one side of a piece of paper from the other.

As with much of the rest of the new humanism, this attempt to place the emotions in their proper perspective, to recognize their importance, and to include them in our picture of the whole man, is not new. Nietzsche inveighed against the attempts by the philosophers, beginning with the early Greeks, to exclude every aspect of man except the rational from the truth-finding process. For Nietzsche, thought without passion was another road to decadence. Kierkegaard, too, attacked the thinker's speculative detachment from life, a quality which had been held to be the highest value in the tradition of Western philosophy. That neither Nietzsche nor Kierkegaard delivered the death blow to the passionless philosophers is all too evident. Behaviorism today is strong and healthy. Herman Kahn and his confreres are able with equanimity to speak of "overkill" and "megadeaths" during the day and go home at night and sip fine wine at their estates along the Hudson. Man, it would seem, has elevated his machines to the status of gods, with the computer their chief, and is seeking to make himself over in their image.

At this point I would like to say a word or two about some of the differences between the traditional forms of humanism—particularly as they are met in the world of education, especially the college and university, but also in the lower schools—and the humanism that I call new. Both, basically, refer to a system of belief which holds that man should rely on his own resources in his search for Truth (or Knowledge or Beauty or God). Both reject the idea that God is the only source of knowledge about reality. Both are interested in man as a growing, unfolding being—as are all philosophies. Apart from this, however, I believe there are some major and critical differences.

One of these is the question of what man is. Remembering that I am speaking of traditional humanism as it appears in education, I believe that it sees man as basically flawed, an uncut diamond, perhaps, needing careful shaping by an outside agent to achieve his highest potential. The new humanists, on the other hand, see man as basically sound, containing in himself, as it were, the pattern for his own becoming—for reaching his own highest potential. They do not see the need for an outside agent to act as shaper. What they find necessary is a supportive environment. This is an important difference—indeed, it shows up in radically different approaches to education, as we shall see later.

Another difference is that traditional humanism is a purely western European phenomenon. It ignores what has taken place in other parts of the world. For the traditional humanists, civilization began with the Greeks and spread through Rome, Italy, France, Germany, and Great Britain. Though it may have penetrated to other parts of the world by now, in small amounts, this small area is still for the traditional humanists the historical world. The rest is to a greater or lesser extent *terra incognita*. It would be a mistake, however, to suppose that traditional humanists think they have left out the rest of the world. What they say—what some of them have said to me, at any rate—is that man is the same, he is man, the world over. If we know about western European man, we therefore know about Man. Furthermore, since western European man exemplifies civilization at its highest, he also exemplifies man at his highest. The seeming differences in man as he is manifested throughout the world (and this does not mean differences such as skin color, kinkiness of hair, etc., but ways of behavior, philosophical tendencies) can be traced to local custom, so to speak. Therefore an African with his strange-seeming ways, an Indian Buddhist with his strange-seeming ways, and a Chinese Taoist with his strange-seeming ways, are only people basically like us exhibiting local ways of being. It may be that they have not achieved the advanced state of being that we have, by virtue of our being members of the western European community with its magnificent heritage, but given time and our example they, too, may aspire to that goal. Therefore, we do not have to study their ways to know what man is. We already know what man is by studying ourselves. Look here, your humanist professor friend is likely to say to you, we are interested in Universals. We want to know rules of behavior which are applicable to man everywhere. We are not interested in this group or that group's unique ways— except as it expands our understanding of man's foibles. Do we not find that all groups have the family, that they fight wars, that there are universal incest taboos, that all peoples have religions, and so on? Obviously, then, these are universal manifestations of what man is. It is these universals which help us to understand man.

The wonderful thing about such an approach is its logic. If you agree that it is universals which take the measure of man, then you are led unerringly to the position that all of man's quaint and inventive ways of expressing these universals are mere decorativeness, so to speak, and it becomes your task to look beyond them, to see the uniformity in the diversity. This is, in fact, what many of the early anthropologists did. They went into the field with their taxonomies of family, kinship, taboo, religion, and carefully fitted what they saw into the grid. Small matter if it did not fit naturally; if it must fit it was made to fit. The consequence, of course, was that we discovered that these various primitive peoples did, indeed, have the same universal needs and morés that we did but that, to the degree that they were difficult to fit into the grid, they were more primitive, less developed, than we.

In marked contrast, for the new humanism, all the parts of the world and all groups figure relevantly. I suppose you might say that in contrast to the deductive approach of tradition, the new humanists approach the question of universals inductively. Instead of setting up a scheme and then trying to fit into it any new experience or information, the new humanists are more interested in looking at new experience and information and working with it to see if any universal tendencies are discernible. If we are to learn to know Man, we must look at him as he appears, and not summarily omit this group or that, or arbitrarily decide what man is and then gather data to support that decision. For the new humanist, knowing that man is shaped by his environment just as he shapes it, and that our culture determines us just as we determine our culture, means that he must take into consideration many things which might otherwise seem irrelevant.

In education, the difference between these two approaches is quite clear. The aim of education for both traditional and new humanism is the development of the individual to his highest potential. Once we have said this, however, we must look at what it means in these two different contexts. In traditional humanism the doctrine of original sin, so to speak, governs the ideas of education. One comes into the world a savage, little more than an animal. To attain the level of being truly "human" demands training. To become educated, to develop to one's highest potential, requires the help of an outside agency. The concept, if I may use another metaphor, is similar to that embodied in the formal garden: the basic raw material is taken by the craftsman, pruned, shaped, trained and polished until it reaches the highest state to which its potential enables it to aspire. This assumes that the natural development of the plants will be irrational, unattractive, and in some subtle way inferior—though this inferiority may not be expressed explicitly.

In this view, then, there must be an outside agent, a craftsman, a master, who knows the forms and the tools, and whose task it is to help shape the plants to these desireable forms. Education requires, among other things, adherence by the student to strict standards of learning and scholarship—standards set by the craftsman, the master. "Rigorous discipline" is a term which finds much use in traditional humanist education. One of the criteria of the development of the individual is his ability to favorably meet these strict standards which are customarily spoken of as inhering in the subjects, whereas it is rather more likely to be the case that they are set by the masters. The main task for education as seen by the traditional humanists has been to take man from his natural, rough state and shape and nurture him into Man, the thinker, the culture-maker. Man—that is, man realizing his highest potential—is thus a product of culture and civilization and a denial of natural tendencies.

The traditional humanistic education emphasizes the development of the student's linguistic ability and his ability to think logically, and seeks to provide him with a set of values and a sense of style. These are the attributes of "civilized" man. Humanism, true to its roots in man's early infatuation with reason and intellect, looks for its highest values in a development as distant from "natural man" as is possible.

Traditional humanistic education places its faith in outside authority and its respect to the legacy of the past. The new humanism, while acknowledging the debt we owe to the past, focuses on the present and the future, and places increased reliance and trust on the student as initiator of the learning process and evaluator of its results. It also admits to the educational process the non-cognitive aspects of growth. The teacher becomes less a master and more a helper. Rather than being the one with the answers he is someone who can help formulate the questions, help find the way to the answers. Answers to what? To the students' questions. Tolstoy said that "every instruction ought to be only an answer to a question put by life"; it is that kind of question which is important in the education of the new humanism, rather than those which have been prepared by the teacher or his surrogate, based on the answers he already has.

"All education begins with a question asked by one eager to learn." Not only does it begin there, but it must end in the same place, namely with the one eager to learn. The learning process— also known as education—cannot end at the end of the professor's grading pencil. As soon as that happens the professor takes the responsibility for what is learned, not the student. It is only meaningless education which needs the professor's evaluation, for what is meaningful is continually evaluated by the learner, who furthermore does not need the goad of grades to motivate him to learn. What he does need, of course, is the experience of evaluating his own learning and his own behavior. This experience he cannot get if the professor takes all the responsibility for the quality of his work, leaving him with only the responsibility to satisfy the professor's demands. Carl Rogers, in discussing elements essential to what he calls "experiential learning," notes that it is self-initiated and that it is evaluated by the learner. Its essence is meaning—meaning for the learner.

All of this does not imply, however, the obsolescence of the teacher. What it does mean is that his role is changed, or, one might even say, he has dropped his role (where role means playing a part other than one's real self) and is now free to be himself. The existential teacher, the humanistic teacher, is an authentic human being interacting with other authentic human beings, all of them with the goal of facilitating human development and personal autonomy. The teacher has become one who facilitates significant learning on the part of the teacher and the student.

In this interactive education which the new humanism calls for, evaluation by the teacher would be further rendered unnecessary by the nature of the interaction. A continuing, nonthreatening feedback process would be in operation, giving both the teacher and the student more valuable, meaningful evaluation of the process. What students want from their teachers in terms of evaluation is not a grade—whether pass/fail or A-B-C-D-F—but rather a human response to them as human beings, and to their ideas. Students need confirmation that they matter as human beings. Thus, a teacher who tells a student that he is uncomfortable because the student does not seem to be making any effort to do anything is communicating much more than one who waits till the end of the semester to give the student a fail or an F, for he is, in effect, opening the possibility for a response from the student. This response may bring to light the reasons for the student not working, which may well be that the subject is not meaningful for him. An F does not invite the student to respond with his own feelings—all he can do is appeal the decision. Appealing is just not communicating. It is begging for acceptance, and is degrading to the student.

Most important in the educational world of the new humanism is community. Since man does not exist alone, and since all his progress—individually or in the mass—is related to his human environment, it would only be natural that his education should also acknowledge this fact. Thus, more than is the case presently, education will be an interactive process, not in the traditional way of formal committees and homogeneous groups, but in the way of students and teachers talking about things, arguing, working together to achieve some goal, working separately when that is appropriate, moving, interacting. In this instance, also, the absence of external evaluation is beneficial. External evaluation—grading by the teacher—pits the students against the teacher and against each other. In such a system it is not to one's advantage to work for the benefit of the class as a whole. In such a situation a spirit of community arises only with great difficulty. The emphasis on community needs the elimination of the external

grade. In essence, then, what the new humanism means in education is an emphasis on the human aspects of man, not just the
cognitive. Man includes the cognitive but the cognitive does not
define man. This emphasis on man as a human being, admitting
the relevance of the affective domain, means that there will be
a de-emphasis on grades; more trust will be placed in the student
to make decisions concerning his own life; teachers will increasingly become facilitators and will be valuable not by virtue of
their superiority in some subject area, but by their experience as
human beings. Subject matter, while containing much of the
traditional, will be included or excluded on the basis of relevance
to the lives of the students and teachers.

One final word about education based on the learner rather
than the subject matter. The fear is sometimes expressed that if
the development of the person is to be the goal, we will end up
with a lot of self-actualized ignoramuses. There are many reasons
why I believe this fear is unfounded, including evidence from
schools where this very kind of education is taking place. The
strongest reason not to be thus fearful, though, is the fact that
people have always learned about things which mattered to them
—things which, in effect, fulfilled them. The great mathe-
maticians, scientists, historians, artists, musicians, became so because they loved science, mathematics, history, etc. They were not
the students who were required to "take" the subjects regardless
of their own feelings. In most cases these outstanding people
studied, worked in their fields, because it would have been unthinkable for them not to. Their lives acquired meaning as they
worked. What a sad contrast with the tens of thousands of young
lives which are made dreary through being forced to follow in the
same paths which those few trod so joyously. If students—all
students—were given the freedom to explore and discover that
which mattered to them, I can hardly imagine that there would be
any less learning going on; I have no doubt that there would be
more joy in our schools. The problem, unfortunately, is not
whether people will learn, given freedom and accorded respect—
we know nothing of what they will or will not do, for we have
scarcely tried that course. The problem is that we are afraid
to try.

6

Crucial Issues

"Whither the highschools?"—the question has been asked almost from the first days of the movement. It is being asked today; it was being asked in 1955 when I first began to study about the folk highschool. The question always has to do with the changing times, the changing makeup of the population, the increased freedom of the young and their greater affluence. The question of whether the highschool could weather these changes and remain a strong and meaningful institution has always intrigued those within and without the movement.

Throughout all the periods of doubt, the highschool has continued to offer its unique experience and has seemingly lost little of its strength and relevance. If its impact today does not seem as great as in the beginning, it must be remembered that the idea is not so radical today as it was then. The sheer numbers of people today and the mass of events occurring each day would tend to make the highschools' influence—even the very fact of their existence—less visible. As to the importance and relevance of their work, the words of Kristen Kold seem as appropriate today as they were over a century ago:

> At Rødding school they work for Danish culture against German culture, and when the former is triumphant the task of that school will have passed; at Hindholm they work for the rights of the peasants, and when the peasants have gained the upper hand, there will be no further use for Hindholm school. But in my school we work for Life as against Death, and that work must continue as long as the world exists.[1]

If the highschools continue the work of Kold's school, they cannot become less relevant, for surely if ever there was a period when the work was for Life as against Death, it is in these days.

In a way, it might be said that it is just this work which today is causing the greatest controversy in the folk highschools. For it is one thing to "work for Life as against Death," and another

---

[1] Noelle Davies, *Education for Life* (London: Williams & Norgate, 1931), p. 119.

to agree on just what that work is. And agreement there is not today in highschool circles. The question manifests itself in the students' increasing expectations of having a voice in the decisions made concerning their educations. It is the question of student participation, student influence, and the teachers' parallel expectations of a more influential voice in the affairs of the school.

The traditional Grundtvigian school, run by the benevolent but authoritarian principal who makes the decisions affecting the lives of the students and teachers alike, is being threatened by the expectations of both teachers and students for more influence in the running of the school. More schools are being run on this more democratic basis, which means that the authoritarian principals and schools are finding themselves under pressure. The social rules are also changing. Whereas, when I stayed at the highschools rules forbade visiting in the rooms of students of the opposite sex—at Askov except for Sunday afternoons, and at Elsinore after ten at night—at many schools today there is no specific rule on the subject, the expectation being that students will behave themselves and that one's own freedom should at no time infringe on the freedom of others.

Some schools are instituting student participation in the leadership of the schools. In some schools there is a one-man, one-vote policy, which includes principal, students, teachers, kitchen girls, etc. At others the students have equal responsibility with the faculty and administration concerning social rules and an advisory status concerning the curriculum.

At the same time there are schools where the principals, though they believe in democracy and "support student participation," reserve the right to limit that democracy and participation to the less important aspects of the school's life. As one principal put it: "There must be a student senate at a highschool, but the students' influence must clearly be limited to what they are qualified for." Other principals may be less fearful of the limits of the students' qualifications, but are haunted by the thought that each group of students will have wildly differing ideas of what a highschool education is, and thus the school will not be the same from one term to the next.

In other statements made recently by highschool principals, one finds a deep pessimism as to man's very nature—a pessimism which, incidentally, seems to run quite counter to Grundtvig's optimistic belief in the common man. One principal, in defending, as he thought, the folk highschools against criticism that they might lead to young people questioning authority, neatly sand-wiched left wing agitators and the escapist tendencies of many of today's youth into a unique statement:

> We, who have the responsibility for the highschools now, have our-selves once been so young that in the name of progress we wanted to turn development back to Romanticism. But we were fortunate in having elders who left us in peace. [He refers here to his claim elsewhere in his article that the students are not responsible for their actions but are being used by outside political agitators—left wing agitators.] . . . Every folk highschool takes its little share of the behavior problems, of people in the process of re-socialization, people recovering after psychic breakdowns, people who because of internal injuries are temporarily hostile toward everyone and everything. And it may soon occur to the authorities that practi-cally every "highschool disturbance" begins when people who have been unbalanced by the times—and not the highschool—protest against being dragged out of their escapism and brought into the twentieth century's problems.[2]

I must hasten to explain here that part of this principal's attack is directed against doctors and psychiatric clinics, who often advise patients who have suffered psychological damage to attend a folk highschool as part of their return to society, after they have made their recovery. It may well be argued that the presence at any school of people who are recovering from more or less severe emotional problems will make the operation of the school more difficult by the mere fact that these people have moved out of the common rut and have glimpsed the human procession, as it were, from outside. There is no doubt that such people might bring to the school a more questioning attitude toward tradition and authority and a stronger-than-average need to find personal meaning in what they do. Such a student might

---

[2] Gustaf Bengtsson, "Fejltolkning af Ryslingestriden!" ("Misinterpretation of the Ryslinge Affaire!"), *Højskolebladet*, XCIII, No. 39 (1968), pp. 645–646.

seem disruptive, but I detect in the statement more than a hint of superiority from the principal. It is obvious that he has never tried to escape the twentieth century's problems!

I would like to quote one more principal in this matter of allowing the students more freedom, partly because I believe it is necessary that the picture of the highschools I present be as honest as possible, and partly because that is, really, one of the questions which looms largest today for any educational institution. In attacking the permissiveness and progressivism which is showing up even in the world of the folk highschool, a principal stated that:

> Man's selfishness, his self-loving and warlike nature are so obviously facts that one can reasonably question a great deal of today's psychological and pedagogical dogma.[3]

Where does all this fit in with Grundtvig and his belief in the common man? Is the "traditional Grundtvigian highschool," (and these principals are absolutely sure that they represent this tradition) really in line with Grundtvig's own thoughts? There is no doubt that Kristen Kold and many of those who came after him left their imprint on the highschool. It may well be that those sturdy and stern men who brought the folk highschool movement into being followed Grundtvig's words in a manner which he might not have foreseen. We must remember that he was principally a poet and dreamer; he did not have to go into the classroom and strike a spark in the breasts of those students. Had he been actively engaged in the classroom it may be that his view of man would have been more somber. There is no way to know, of course. We do know that he thought about the role of the schoolmaster, however, and wrote about it as follows:

> We know well that the old crochety schoolmaster still sticks with us, even if we have given up the paryk which went with the role, so that we think it is best for the young people that they listen piously to everything we say and repeat exactly after us; but we must learn to recognize that that absolutely does not fit at a *folkelig* Highschool, which the young people are neither driven to with threats or lured to with earning power, but will only visit and

---

[3] Morten Bredsdorff, "Democrati og Demokratisme," Højskolebladet, XCIII, No. 40 (1968), 666.

value if they find it both relevant and enjoyable, and whether they will find it thus none can say but themselves, so for that end they must be given a meaningful opportunity in the school council, and whatsoever they, so to speak, are unanimously dissatisfied with can in certain circumstances be very good, but it doesn't belong at a *folkelig* Highschool.[4]

The clash between the conservative way of looking at the highschool's role and what might be called a more progressive approach, is exemplified by a series of events which took place in 1968, at the highschool founded by Kristen Kold: Ryslinge. The Ryslinge Affair, as it became known, caused much bitter recrimination among highschool people. The affair attracted attention first when, in early July of 1968, five teachers were fired from Ryslinge. This followed some months of disagreement between some of the teaching staff and the principal. The dispute centered around teachers' authority and working conditions, and the firing came immediately upon the heels of an agreement whereby teachers and principal were to work together as best they could for the remainder of the school year.

By the twenty-fourth of July the teachers had been re-hired and fired again, a group of students who had protested the firing of the teachers had been expelled and readmitted, the Minister for Folk Highschools had interrupted his vacation to arbitrate the affair—all with wide publicity in the press and on television. Some of the students boycotted classes as a protest over the second firing of the teachers, but the matter died away when the students left for vacation. The teachers, who were fired, nevertheless continued to teach until the end of the session.

When the students returned from their vacation they held a meeting to discuss the situation. One result of the meeting was that they missed their afternoon classes—they had asked the principal's permission to be excused from their afternoon classes because of the meeting—and the principal declared that those who had missed classes were expelled. At the meeting thirty-four of the fifty-six students continuing in the summer session after the vacation voted to boycott classes in protest against the firing of the teachers.

---

[4] Erik B. Nissen, "Grundtvig on elevdemokrati, studenteroprør, m.v.," Højskolebladet, XCIIII, No. 34 (1968), 560.

In the round of events which followed, the students sought out the Minister of Education with their case; he advised them to return to school and carry on with classes, and also advised the principal to readmit them. The students agreed but the principal insisted that certain of the thirty-two students had to be expelled. At this the entire group decided to leave and moved from the school to a nearby inn. There their number grew to thirty-five. Since it seemed impossible to achieve any working agreement with the principal, the students decided to collect money, hire a school and finish their term. They were able to rent a folk highschool which was on vacation, found a principal whom the Ministry approved so the school could receive government support, and received the volunteer teaching services of a number of writers, teachers, artists, historians and others, each of whom volunteered to teach a class for one day. With some of their money they also hired permanent teachers, and the school finished out the term.

There were responses of many kinds to this unprecedented action by students. The principal of Ryslinge sent a letter to the students' parents warning them that Ryslinge would not stand behind the education they had gotten at Hesbjerg, the other school. He and others pointed suggestively at the fact that some of the people who had volunteered to teach at Hesbjerg were members of the Socialist Left Party. While this was true, what he did not say was that the paid and volunteer teachers represented most shades, if not all, of the political spectrum. Some comments on the affair hailed the actions of the students and praised their initiative.

In an interview in one of Copenhagen's leading newspapers, the principal who decided to work with the students in their attempt to build a school spoke about the students and about freedom and responsibility:

> While everyone hears about the students' freedom, at most high-schools there is a smoothly working system which encourages dependence and irresponsibility. It is difficult to understand how these schools can talk of education for democracy.
>
> It is this system which is the highschool's problem today—and not the disturbances some may resort to to defend themselves against the system. As one school administrator said: "The core of the matter is that at my school the students never needed to resort to the methods they had to use to be listened to at Ryslinge!"

Our group at Hesbjerg consisted of 35 students, who, after having left Ryslinge received the Education Ministry's approval to try their own hand. They did not represent any revolutionary dispositions, but very ordinary young people who, out of ordinary self-respect, found it necessary to confront a totalitarian system. As one student said: "Before, they told us a lot about democracy, now we are trying to live democracy."

It has been unfortunate for this group that some have characterized it as hoodlums and others as angels and heroes. It is neither of these. [He goes on to explain that the student council had the responsibility for housekeeping, purchasing, curriculum, cash and book-keeping and agreements with outside lecturers, and he comments.]

When students work with the large problems in the running of a school, they go to work with impressive seriousness and thoroughness. This stands in marked contrast to the garrulity with which they work with less important things such as parties, smoking in classes or dishwashing duties. This may be of some interest to those principals who have only allowed their students to work with the less important questions and consequently don't dare leave the meaningful ones to them. A serious job with serious things can only be learned if one works with the serious things.

Maybe one day we will reach the point where the highschool's free mode of operation (and it is *still* free in principle) preferably is used to teach the young that work and discussion in themselves provide for development. Therefore, no matter is too small for one to devote some time to it. Something quite decisive happens to a person when he grapples with a problem—whatever that problem happens to be.[5]

I have pieced together this account of the events from many sources. Both sides granted newspaper interviews and wrote letters to papers and journals. Outsiders, too, had their opinions, which were freely available and widely differing. It may be of interest that throughout the entire affair the principal of Ryslinge was solidly supported by the board of trustees of the school, the alumni association, the mayor and the local newspaper. Whatever it was he did, and the students' and teachers' complaint was that he ran the school in a high-handed and capricious manner—of which we got glimpses as the events unfolded—he had the backing of the community.

The students themselves, quite apart from any genius or cour-

---

[5] Johs. Dragsdahl, in an interview in *Politiken,* Copenhagen, Denmark, (September 25, 1968).

age they may have had, were extremely fortunate. First, they were able to find a place to hold school and, even more important, a principal who not only had the time but believed in what they were doing. Then, they had the good fortune to embark on their educational adventure in a country where education is carefully supported by the government, and where the Minister of Education himself backed the justice of their cause, and thus enabled them to retain the government support which they needed to pay the teachers at their new school.

Ryslinge did not fall. The principal is still there. Other classes of students have come and gone with no more revolts. There are other schools where there exists a "guided democracy," where the principal, sometimes in concert with the teachers, makes the important decisions and the students are urged to participate in planning the parties and entertainments. That is, after all, the traditional way. And even if the democratic aspects of the tradition may seem somewhat slender, and though independence may be discouraged in such a situation, it is undeniably from this very tradition that the many valuable contributions from the folk highschools have come. It would be a mistake to condemn these traditional principals and their schools out of hand. A more realistic way to look at it might be to acknowledge that the traditional forms grew out of social situations and were valid responses to them, but that present conditions are such that democracy in education has, in fact, assumed new meanings, including the students' right to participate in the decisions which affect them educationally.

There are schools which are taking the idea of student participation seriously and experimenting in the direction of more responsibility for those affected most directly by the education. Perhaps the most radical experiments are taking place not at folk highschools, but at the so-called continuation schools. These schools are very similar in goals and methods to folk highschools, the main difference being in the age group they serve—from fourteen to eighteen years. They, too, are boarding schools, and to a great extent follow the folk highschool philosophy. Being a newer phenomenon without the long tradition of the highschools, often having younger teachers and principals, they may find it easier to be experimental and adventurous. Even so, they have not been able to experiment without paying the price. More than one principal has been replaced by the school's board of trustees because he "went too far" in granting freedom, in trying to extend the democratic process to the students. Even as I write this, the school whose program I wish to describe, is experiencing problems between conservative and progressive elements in its directorship.

At Rantzausminde the students have been involved in the work of the school to a degree not often found elsewhere. The school's highest authority in almost all areas is a general meeting which includes everyone who is connected with the school: students, kitchen girls, principal and teachers—and which works on the principle of one man, one vote. If the general assembly wants to, it may set up a student council which acts as the general assembly's agent, but the general assembly, where everyone has an equal voice, is the heart of the plan. In the area of curriculum, only the first days of the term are planned in advance. After that, the general assembly takes over.

Of course, in such an undertaking as that at Rantzausminde, there must be a great deal of trust—trust in others, but not least of all, trust in oneself. At a meeting of Free School ° people recently, one of the teachers from Rantzausminde answered questions about the problems in running such a school. With respect to what one could expect from the young people, he replied that

---

° According to the Danish Constitution, parents are not required to send their children to a public elementary school, but are bound to see that they get an education not inferior to that provided by the public elementary school. (A provision that many see as being influenced by the folk highschools.) As a result, there are a number of non-examination cooperative elementary schools. These Free Schools are usually started by the parents of the children and often represent distinctive pedagogical or religious viewpoints: they are often associated with highschools and with former highschool students who wish for their children the same freedom in education they experienced at the highschool. Others are associated with the Grundtvigian wing of the Lutheran church, the Free Congregations.

The schools are quite free and as a rule are not supervised by the local authorities. They can choose their own inspector whose duty is limited to seeing that the instruction in Danish, written and oral, writing and arithmetic is satisfactory. The other subjects of the public elementary school must also be taught, but the principal has sole responsibility for the quality of this instruction.

The schools receive grants from the government—up to 80% of a public schoolteacher's salary for the teachers and 50% of the money it would cost to keep a child in a regular school. Thus, while the government, in effect, makes the Free Schools possible, the parents must still provide the initial money for acquiring the school building and must make a small, but by no means insignificant, continuing financial commitment. Today there are about 175 Free Schools, with about ten thousand students, in a country of less than five million.

their experience was that if you expected little of the students they would give you little. If you expected them to act intelligently and take responsibility—not the sort like planning a weekend dance or the decorations for a party, but meaningful responsibility—they would do their best to oblige. If one shows trust in them, he added, they will be trustworthy.

In answer to the question of whether a power struggle took place—a question which seemed to be in the minds of many of the participants—he answered that many students came to the Free School from a society which mistrusted everything connected with law and order—and whose fault is that, he asked. At the beginning it is difficult to get the students to enter into a cooperative undertaking, he said, but "that is precisely our job: to develop that desire in them." [6]

We see here the grounds on which the battle for the highschool's future will be fought. As the young people begin to find themselves, they are demanding more and more a meaningful part in the decisions concerning their lives. As they become more aware of their powers and their value as persons, they are demanding more autonomy and more influence in their education, including a highschool education. As they daily see more clearly the mistakes of their elders—mistakes such as wars and poverty and racial discrimination—and as they become ever more certain in their refusal to acquiesce in perpetuating these mistakes, their demands will grow both in strength and in scope.

If the highschools are effective in carrying out what has actually been one of their missions throughout the years—that of awakening the young people to their own potentiality—they will actually be forcing themselves to change. For it is only if the schools *fail* in this task that they will be able to continue in the old paths, relatively aloof to the outside world, seeing their role as that of parent surrogate gently but firmly shaping the youth of this generation. It might be said that success means change— change to meet the changing demands of the students as they grow and become more aware of themselves. A young highschool teacher angrily replied to allusions to his leading the young people

---

[6] "Demokrati i skolen" (Democracy in the school), *Højskolebladet,* XCIII, No. 41 (1968), p. 684.

astray: "I am neither a leader-astray of youth nor a leader of youth. The young people's revolt comes from the young people themselves. I want to educate people who are radical, not train them to become radicals. I believe that at any given moment it is radicals the society needs."

It takes a good deal of trust in young people—in people in general—to want to educate radicals. For one of the things radicals do is stir things up, agitate for change. How can we be sure the change will be for the better, or that it will not disrupt our own lives? If we trust people, we can make the assumption that whatever changes they agitate for will be in the best interests of themselves and us. So it is not enough that we trust them. We must also trust ourselves. We must assume that we, ourselves, are trustworthy, that what we are doing is, to the best of our knowledge, beneficial to all involved, is in the best interests of them and ourselves. Even more important, we must have the conviction that as we are honorable—or at least strive to be so—so the same must be true of most of our fellow men. This is not to say that there are not men who, on an operational, day to day basis, can fairly be described as dishonest, even evil. Neither is it to say, in effect, that I, in my dealings with others, have been honest and generous in my dealings with these dishonest others, who are only waiting to cheat me. It seems to me that the essence of self-trust, self-respect, is the ability to discriminate in individual cases, so that one is not constantly on his guard against others, but is able to be on guard when it is appropriate.

Trust is a key word in education. It was one of the cornerstones in the original idea of a highschool for the ordinary people, as it occurred to Grundtvig. It is perhaps, a cornerstone of the new humanism. There is no doubt that it is an essential ingredient in the culture of the young. Yet, lack of trust seems to characterize many of the educational plans of the present and the future, and of course much of what occupies the time of both students and teachers in our schools today is work entailed by a system which does not trust the students. (This is not to say that the students can or cannot be trusted—though obviously I believe they can, and must be.)

The matter of trust may well turn out to be crucial in the future of the folk highschool movement. Just as the student of today differs from his nineteenth-century predecessor with respect to the amount of information he brings to school, his attitudes, and his appearance, so have the requirements for trust changed. Kold, for example, trusted his students. But he did not trust them to be able to determine the curriculum, even in part. He did not trust them to set their own bed hours or the like. In his day, the young people did not expect that kind of trusting.

Today, trust seems to demand more of one. The area covered by trusting, one might say, has increased drastically. Today many young people expect to be trusted in matters where their parents and grandparents expected to be mistrusted. When this expected trust is not forthcoming, the more self-aware of these young people find themselves in the position of demanding trust. Such demands are likewise a break in the tradition and the consequence is often hostility and friction. In the Ryslinge affair, one of the things which the young people were demanding was to be trusted more. The principal not only could not give this trust, but the very fact that the students were expecting it—demanding it—apparently was so unthinkable to him that he was unable to react with anything but force. That is, he ejected them from the school.

Not all young people are making this demand. Not all young people see themselves as being competent to make the major decisions governing their own lives. In this way they are like most of us adults. Many do not believe that they yet have the right to demand their rights. After all, there has been only one Ryslinge Affair—no other highschools have had student revolts.

Yet, I believe it is fair to say that the youth are beginning to expect to be trusted. Part of their reason for this is the feeling among many of them that the older generation is not to be trusted. Many young people, when they look at the world they are inheriting, cannot help but exclaim: "The adults are not to be trusted to run things. Our ideas are at least as valid as theirs. We must begin to trust ourselves rather than them."

One of the problems in trying to make the folk highschool appealing to the young people in the city has been the residential nature of the school. While it is in the nature of agricultural work that the winter is a more slack time, with the great periods of activity occurring in the spring, summer or fall, with planting and harvesting, the nature of most jobs in the city allows no built-in slack period when the worker could take a five month leave of absence and find his job still waiting for him. However, if the highschool, in order to accommodate itself to the life tempo of the urban youth, were to drop the residential requirement and offer part-day or evening classes, it would be eliminating at the same time one of the most important parts of its offering—the experience of community which grows up among the students and faculty.

The workers' highschools have decided the question by retaining the residence feature; they are boarding schools, like other highschools, to which students go between jobs, or on a leave of absence from their jobs. No doubt the fact of the schools being run by the Workers' Educational Association aids in getting such leaves of absence for the students. In 1916 Borup's Highschool was founded in Copenhagen in an attempt to meet the workers on their own ground. It was not a residential school, but in all other respects, methods, courses, and philosophy, it was a real highschool. The school has had at least a moderate success over the years. While it has not spawned a score of similar schools, it at least has remained in action, and is still operating in Copenhagen.

An experiment is being tried in Sweden which may point the way to a slightly different solution of the residence problem. A number of highschools which have traditionally been located in the country have set up daughter schools in nearby cities. At the present time there are about thirty such schools, often quite large. Typical of these daughter schools is the one in Göteborg, which is part of the folk highschool at Kungälv. The school at Göteborg has 110 students, divided into three classes, while the mother school at Kungälv has 70, in one class. The building for the school in Göteborg is provided by the city, which also is responsible for all the costs of the building's operation and maintenance. The cost to the students is nothing, as all education in Sweden is free.

The student body at Göteborg, which is probably typical of the filial or daughter schools, is on the average slightly older than ordinary highschool students. Since most of them are there to get an education which they weren't able to get earlier, most tend to come from a lower economic level than the typical highschool student. A new trend is the attendance of housewives who are not working. In the Swedish highschools in general there is a greater emphasis on practical training and on "solid" subject mattei, and this is reflected by the filials. Many of those attending Göteborg are working to obtain certification as recreation workers, and the school offers a course leading to the certificate. Some of the students, however, come solely to get that unique experience which a folk highschool provides. About twenty per cent of them come as part of the government's retraining program.

Emphasis in the school's curriculum is on those subjects which have to do with helping people: psychology, sociology, philosophy, organizational behavior. Music is also offered. As lectures are wanted often, many are scheduled. For many students the first contact with a folk highschool comes as a distinct shock. Many of them come from a generation which is used to absolute schedules, inflexible courses of study, and at the highschool they are presented with *suggestions* for their schedule, *suggestions* as to what courses they might take, etc. But they are highly motivated, and in this atmosphere of free learning, are able to make the best use of their interests.

The students also have an important part in shaping the course of the school. Each week representatives from the different classes meet with the teachers in an open meeting. All present have a voice, but only the elected representatives may vote on decisions. The students determine the activities of the school from the contents of the brochure to the contents of the courses. The only area in which they have no say is that of the final presentation—a written or oral presentation which is the culmination of their semester's work. This presentation is one of the criteria upon which their admission to further study is based.

Because the schools lack the residence feature which is such an integral part of the ordinary highschool experience, everything is done to build a sense of community with the given situation. A great emphasis is placed on group activities such as theater evenings, excursions and field trips. Barriers between teachers and students are removed as much as possible. The teachers have no separate lounge where they can retreat during lunch hour or between classes. All members of the school have a key, so that they may use the building at any time of the day or night. One of the consequences is that the students come to think of the school as a place to be, a place to come. Some come to take advantage of the TV, which many do not have where they live in the city, and they prefer to be at the school rather than hanging around a café.

The fact that there are now thirty of these filial schools seems to argue for the timeliness of the idea. The school at Göteborg reports that there are always more applicants than they can accept, though the school has been in existence only two years. These schools offer to the city dweller something which the traditional highschools have been less able to offer; an environment in which to pursue the goal of becoming more educated, in which there is the freedom and flexibility, the sharing of responsibility, which just does not exist at many folk highschools, and to which many of the people are accustomed in their daily lives. In this respect I believe the Danish highschools have found a greater gap between what they have to offer and what the city dweller wants and needs. For the Danish schools have through the years been more characterized by an emphasis on character-building, on the Grundtvigian traditions, on the old way of doing things. Since this tradition was also the tradition of rural Denmark, the kind of experience they offered was very congenial to the youth from rural areas. City youth, however, seem to care less for traditions, have looser ties with the church, and more interest in the present, the future, and practical things.

This situation has been clearly recognized by the Danish highschool people and it has caused a great deal of troubled discussion. For, as sincerely as it was felt that the highschools should try to establish contact with the young people of the city, equally sincere was a reluctance to break with the traditions of the past, the traditions which in many cases had made the highschools the strong moral force they have been. Today, with younger men coming into the leadership roles in highschool circles, men who did not know the old time greats of the highschools and who never listened to their inspiring lectures, there is a greater sense of experimentation. Krogerup Highschool was established primarily for the bright young leaders in the worker movement. It was, so to speak, the folk highschool for young radicals. But in saying that, I must point out that it was not the intent of the highschool to *make* radicals. The radicals already existed, in the persons of the young people who saw the need for wide-reaching reforms. The role of the highschool—of the radical highschool—was to give these young radicals a chance to participate in the highschool experience; to have the experience of working on their education in a community of others who were also working on theirs; to experience the exciting feeling of doing something with others because it was what they wanted to do—when there was no raise or step up in the job hierarchy, or another certificate as a result. Finally, the radical highschool was important because those who started it believed that there was something in the highschool experience—nothing supernatural, but very hard to describe—which made people more human. The radical highschool, then, might be said to exist to mix the young people's radicalism with some humanism, for the sake of society.

Still, the Swedish experiment with filial schools is a new step. I believe there are good reasons to hope that it will signal a new era in the development of that truly humanistic institution, the folk highschool. Today, people as never before are sensing the need of man to live and work in groups. Communes are being formed by young and old alike. Some are doomed to failure from the very start, but all are a response to what is a very basic need of the human being, a need which we seem only recently to have rediscovered. This search for the benefits of community are leading the young people to found their own free universities and experimental colleges, where the concept of free contribution and free access are the backbone, and where there is a real sense of involvement and community among the participants.

In this atmosphere, I see an experiment such as the filial school moving naturally and organically into some sort of an open-ended residence college or highschool, where students will be free to come and live as they feel the need, and free to move out as they feel the need to move on. And all the time, the school itself will be a living thing, filled with the life and energies of those associated with it. I cannot help but believe that today the young people themselves are sending a message to the people of the highschools, a message which is loud and clear: we are looking for new meanings to life; we are looking for new modes of living. We are looking for questions and we are looking for answers to questions we haven't asked and can't ask. We are trying to make this journey.

Do you want to come with us? But you cannot come on your terms. You need not come on our terms. We all come without terms, without preconditions. Come with us or be left behind.

This, more or less, is the crossroads where we find the high-schools today. The pace of change has increased. No more do we have time to retreat into our traditions and see what will happen. In a real sense, it is a case of come with us or be left behind.

7

Implications

> ... in my school we work for
> Life as against Death, and
> that work must continue as
> long as the world exists.
>
> Kristen Kold

If we believe that the new humanist picture of man comes closest to what man "really" is, then it seems incumbent upon us to find some alternatives to our present system of values, especially in education. The kind of education offered today in the United States is not appropriate for the kind of person the new humanism describes.

I believe that Danish folk highschool experience supports the picture of man as the new humanism describes him. It also offers rich material to use in trying to develop something more appropriate for his education. The success of the highschools, as measured both by the response of their former students and by the influence they have had on the society, seems to argue that the type of person described by the new humanism exists and that certain approaches to education are appropriate to his development.

With few exceptions, our schools today do not encourage the students toward self-actualization or self-fulfillment. If we allow education to continue in the same paths it is now traveling, we will never know what man is capable of because he will never have the chance to really become himself. The system requires him to expend a great amount of energy becoming what someone else wants. This implies that there is someone who knows what the young person should be and what is best for him. This is a myth. The state of the world today should be evidence enough that we do not know what is good for ourselves or young people. The older generation does not know, except in very general terms, what is good for the younger generation. It is time we gave up this myth that we, the teachers, know what is best for the students.

99

This does not mean that we must abdicate all responsibility. We do have experience, we do have some idea of what is good or bad for *us*. We have some idea of what it is like—for us—to be alive, to be adult, to be male or female, or to be any of the myriad things we are. If we are honest we also know something about the ways we feel life has short-changed us, the areas of our lives and our selves which seemed to shrivel and die.

Our job as teachers is not to say to youth, "You must be like us." It is to offer ourselves and our experiences as examples of what it can be like to *be*. If our lives have been full, we are an example of the rewards of a full life—indeed, we can show how to live a full life, if we are living it. If our lives have been cramped and frustrating, we can show the evil effects of denying our humanity. If we are authentic, if we are honorable, the young people will accept our offer and honor it. They will accept it and use what they are able to or what they need for the purpose of making themselves. But we must not expect them to accept everything we offer or to become like us.

It is here that a teacher can best serve; it is here that his students can become more than he is. If we say, "Be like me," we limit them to what has been. If, however, we can say, "Be what you will become," the way is opened for growth which we may be unable even to dream of.

Therefore, if we are to free youth to become all that they might be, we must free them from our expectations. We must also free them from the enormous waste engendered by a system which requires most of their energies to be expended in becoming something other than what they are, something planned in the central office.

This means that we must also hope to free them from the prospect of the mechanistic school of the future, where their every move is planned by someone other than themselves, and their ultimate growth is tied to what someone else has been able to program into a computer. I believe that this becomes even more important when we discover that those who decide these ultimate ends are experimental psychologists, businessmen, and computer specialists. Even were this approach to education a valid human one, the planners should be poets, artists, musicians, impractical dreamers; people whose life work is life. But to have one's life planned by an experimental psychologist . . .

The question is asked, "Do you advocate starting a folk high-school here in the U.S.?" The answer is no. It has been tried, with a great lack of success. This is not what we have to gain from a study of the highschools. Rather, what we can learn by looking at what the schools have actually tried to do, how they have tried to do it and the extent to which they have been successful, is that a humanistic education is possible and desirable. I believe that one hundred twenty years of experience demonstrates this assertion abundantly.

As soon as we forget that these are "schools for farmers," or schools for this or schools for that and look, not at the stereotype, but at the schools themselves and what they do, we will find that they are schools for people—for human beings. Then we will be able to say, "If I want a school for human beings, what can I find out from the folk highschool experience about ways in which it might develop?"

What are some of the things in the highschool experience which can be helpful to us in educating human beings?

No Examinations or Diplomas

Though we do not have the external examinations which assert hegemony over the Danish student's life, we do have grades and diplomas. Whatever evils the system of external examinations possesses, equal though different ones are inherent in our system. Both stifle innovation and experimentation by teacher and student alike. Both require the student to please an entire succession of teachers in order to succeed. Neither system belongs in education which is *for* the learner.

The question of eliminating grading is currently under discussion in this country. Surely the evidence from the continuing high-school experiment involving such large numbers of young people is suggestive of the fact that young people, when given the opportunity to learn something meaningful, will learn without the stimulus of grades or diplomas.

Kristen Kold, when asked why his school did not have examinations, and how he knew what his pupils were learning as it did not, replied:

> Of course when you are putting drain pipes in the soil you have to mark the places where you put them. But when you sow grain you need no markers; in the time of harvest you will see the results.

Need it be pointed out that at the time of harvest in our own educational experience, one of the most common fruits is the failure of school bond elections to pass?

Freedom of Attendance

When the only entrance requirement is the desire to learn, those who are interested will attend. When the only entrance requirement is the desire to learn, those who are interested *may* attend. Minority group students here in the U.S. have often found their desire to learn blocked by admission requirements which discriminate against them in one way or another. This touches on what education is supposed to be about. The school is supposed to be a place where those wanting to learn can go and find help. Instead, too often it is a place where those who do not want to be there are forced to remain, while because of overcrowding, admissions officers are continually seeking more sophisticated ways— known as admissions policies— of keeping out those who want to be there but for whom there is no room.

Teachers' Qualifications

A teacher is qualified if he has something to offer to the students. Teachers need to be genuine, full-time people. Degrees and credentials have little to do with whether one is a good teacher.

Acceptance of the Social Nature of Man

Social interaction must be an integral part of the school experience—interaction among students, teachers and as many others as possible. It is possible that parents and others would interest themselves in such schools, and enter into the communal life.

The Learner as the Center
of the Educational Experience

When the attempt is made to offer the things that the learners want and need, it may be found that as the choice becomes free the learner will have more questions, not fewer, and that they will be questions about what is important to him. One result will be that the kinds and range of subjects desired by the students will tend to become ever larger.

Creative Arts

Not only singing, but the other arts, painting, drama, potting, sculpting, dance, etc., will be an integral part of the experience. The school itself must also reflect this attitude toward creative expression as an integral part of the human experience, with the sanctity of the buildings never interfering with the right of the students and the teachers to display their work, or to change their environment. Buildings and surroundings will be beautified organically, by the continuing creative processes within the school and their manifestations rather than by an architect once and for all.

The Curriculum

In general, the curriculum is what we have been talking about. These are the kinds of things which would probably go on at a school for human beings, and the conditions under which they would go on. What will actually go on will depend on the needs and competencies of the teachers and the students. As far as subject matter is concerned, I should think that the list of special classes at Askov would be a good jumping-off place. With this list as a start, surely students and teachers could go on. Since we are including in our school all ages of children instead of just those the folk highschools accept—though we may actually have them in separate divisions, of course—the range of subjects will be commensurately greater. There may be short-term classes in: Why is there dirt on the ground? What makes us stay on the surface of the earth? Where do I come from? These are serious questions and must be answered sooner or later. It may be that older students might wish to share with the younger ones some of their own experiences. We might see a teenager studying up on gravity because a group of small students asked him why their ball always fell down, or some such question, and he realized that he would have to find out more about it himself before he could explain it. We might even see, as I have, a group of teenagers learning from smaller children—a game, a singing rhyme, or just how to be alive.

Classes would be added or dropped as they were needed or ignored, or as the abilities of the teachers dictated. It might be found desirable to have some courses required and the rest elective, or it might be found equally desirable to have all the courses elective. If there are certain "core" courses which are necessary to cope effectively in the society, there may well be a steady demand for them even without requiring them.

I must stress that this is not a purely haphazard situation with students and teachers bouncing from one subject to another with no purpose. The underlying quality of the entire undertaking is purpose, for we are talking about people who are seeking to learn. We must not wrongly conclude, from our contact with our traditional forms of education, that there is no purpose to learning, or that man does not learn of his own free will. Man has been epitomized as many things: the Toolmaker, the Creature who Plays, the Thinker, but not least as the Learner. It is, perhaps, one of the strongest indictments of our traditional education that it is so difficult to think of learning as a natural process, or to look upon learning as a highly purposive activity.

Our supposition, in postulating a school for human beings, is that given two conditions; 1) freedom to attend or not, and 2) a curriculum based on the needs and desires of the students and teachers, the school will be characterized by a sense of purpose and commitment which is entirely lacking in most of the forms of education with which we are acquainted. The folk highschool experience has shown that when students wanting to find out come come together with teachers who want to help them find out, there is purpose and commitment.

Unfortunately, we have never allowed ourselves the freedom, within the system, to test the possibilities of such a thing. Neither did the Danes. The folk highschools started and remained outside the system so they *would* have the freedom to experiment. The example of the students who left Ryslinge last summer demonstrates the advantage of being outside the system. Unfortunately, it also demonstrates the advantage of being outside the system in a culture which not only talks about being committed to education, but does something about it. Just as the Danish society no doubt owes part of its high level of social concern to the influence of the highschools, it is even more true that they owe part of their continued existence to a society which believes in supporting education—both inside and outside the system.

This poses a double question for would-be radicals in education in the U.S. Real experimentation, real initiative, cannot exist within the system. Outside the system, however, there is little or no likelihood for economic support for a radical educational enterprise. What should one do? Should one try to build a radical school within the system, with its advantages, especially monetary, but with limited freedom, or should one try to work outside the system, with the advantage of freedom but the handicap of limited funds? The choice is not an easy one, and may, in fact, not be as black and white as it seems. Surely the truth of the matter is that one cannot neglect either course. For those able to, the experiments outside the system will doubtless prove to provide goals and examples of what results we can expect in a human educational system. For those who must remain inside the system, there is the necessity to work there for a greater commitment to real education, rather than the trappings of education. We are starting late. It may be that a humanistic education can only exist in a humanistic society. In the meantime, there is the hopeful fact that great numbers of students and teachers are discovering that real education does not need large buildings, laboratories, expensive textbooks, and similar trappings. More and more people are voluntarily giving up the outer signs of the affluent society—television, large cars, expensive houses, new clothes, large liquor bills—in order to be able to do the things which really have meaning for them: making things of leather, painting, making music, teaching, learning, growing things. This great movement toward meaningful vocations bodes well for any attempt to establish schools for human beings. As we look around us, in fact, we find such schools coming into existence almost daily, so that now there are hundreds of them, from parents' cooperative nurseries to free high schools.

Paul Goodman and Edgar Friedenberg, among others, have suggested that we do away with our formal education system. In such an eventuality it would be relatively easy to establish a school based on the principles we have been talking about. However, under such conditions the need for such a school would not be nearly as great as it is today. These principles must be applied to education today—whether within the system or without—not at some future date when the educational millenium has arrived. For it is today that they are needed. It is today that students' lives are being wasted in dehumanized schools. It is today that we must heed the despairing cry of the young New York high school girl: "They're wasting our lives!"

Kold's words about there being a need for his school as long as the world exists are a reminder that in our country today there are groups whose position is in some ways similar to that of the Danish peasant in the nineteenth century. The blacks, the Chicanos, the native Americans and other minority groups are seeking to re-establish their ties with their roots—their mother-tongue and their fatherland. In Denmark the peasants may have "gained the upper hand," the Danish culture may have been triumphant over the German culture, but here in the U.S. the battle is just beginning. Our peasants—the minority groups—have *not* gained the upper hand, and their fight for cultural identity is just beginning.

The question we have to ask here is, given the conditions of our day, would a folk highschool type of movement suffice? In the nineteenth century, though the peasants were in a depressed state, time was on the side of the reformers. What could not be done today could be done tomorrow. Change never took place over night. Today, however there is a strong feeling among the reformers that what is not done today may never get done. Almost twenty-five years of living under the threat of nuclear annihilation has erased whatever feelings the nineteenth century had that tomorrow was another day which could be counted on to come. Today we do not have that confidence. What we do have is population growth racing with pollution as the final solution for man if he should restrain himself from committing atomic suicide. For the young we must add to this the draft, which leaves no certainty at all that there will be a tomorrow. When our leaders are assassinated before our very eyes, the feeling increasingly becomes one of the overwhelming necessity for change to occur now.

In this atmosphere, could a folk highschool type of education be useful? There is no clear-cut answer to this question, but I would suggest that the principles on which the highschool is built, the emphasis on the integrity and innate value of the students, are certainly relevant to whatever period we find ourselves in. Our peasants of today, the blacks, the Chicanos, and the other minorities, must be able to achieve their self respect. They are not going to achieve it through the traditional forms of schooling which, in any case, are all too often denied them.

I do not advocate transplanting folk highschools to the U.S. As it developed, the folk highschool was a response to a set of social and political realities as they existed in Denmark between the beginning of the nineteenth century and the middle of the twentieth. In the U.S. in the latter half of the twentieth century the political realities are quite different. The forms which a movement for cultural identity, for the rights of the peasants, for Life as against Death will take under these realities may be vastly different from the folk highschool as we have known it.

However, whatever the outward forms dictated by the conditions under which the movement exists, I am convinced that in any movement which has as its goals those stated by Kold, there must be a central philosophy very similar to that which animated the highschool movement. For that philosophy is essentially humanistic; it takes as its starting point and its end that man is honorable, valuable, that he prefers peace to violence, love to hate, art to war, cooperation to competition. This is the philosophy which made the folk highschool idea so powerful in the beginning and which *must* lie at the core of any movement which seeks to allow man to fulfill his potential, to allow him to become himself, Man. This philosophy is doubly essential today in a world which waits cowering on the brink of destruction. Arthur Combs has said: "We live in a world where humanism is not just a nice, polite sentiment, but an essential for survival." [1]

---

[1] Arthur Combs, "Curriculum Change and the Humanist Movement," *Educational Leadership*, XXIII, No. 7 (1966), 527.

Something is already being done. In Harlem there are store-front schools. In the south there have been and are freedom schools. In the fields of California and other agri-business states there are teachers who are working with the farm workers and, just as in Denmark, there are leaders arising among these people. Students are forming free universities where, without grades or entrance requirements, they are studying about things which concern their lives. Parents are founding free schools where their children may learn the joys of learning rather than merely the frustration. Students are sponsoring teach-ins on the draft, on the war in Vietnam, on ecology. These things are already happening. They are being made to happen by the people themselves. This is one of the differences between the situation today and in nineteenth-century Denmark.

Yet, at the same time, in our high schools students are expelled for having long hair; girls must submit to having their skirts measured to determine whether they are within the limits of the school administration's moral code; conditions in big city schools continue to worsen as a public which hated its own school days refuses to vote adequate funds for its children's education.

It seems obvious that despite the many exciting things happening today in the field of education, for the great majority of young people the educational experience is anything but uplifting, anything but fulfilling, anything but humanizing. The folk highschool is one of the great revolutionary ideas in educational thought. Further, it is more than an idea, it is an accomplished fact. Many see the movement as having been crucial to the direction in which the cultural growth of Denmark has moved. I believe that the same threads which run through that movement and made it great run also through the movement which I have called the new humanism. It seems to me the great lesson we can learn from the highschool experience, and, indeed, the Scandinavian experience as a whole, is that humanism does work as a guiding principle in man's affairs. I suggest that if we want a society based on cooperation, on respect for man, on the individual's right to become all that he has in him to become, the direction we must go, and a direction whose value has been demonstrated beyond a doubt by the folk highschools, is toward freedom. The folk highschool does not require you to attend it; you must come because of something in yourself. Once you make the decision you are not graded on how well you follow someone else's path. At the end you are not given a testament saying that you are now a fully qualified follower of this path or that one. In the most basic sense, you arrive at a high-school with only your self and you leave with only your self. What you have done in the meantime is to have looked at many paths, tried on many ideas, watched the people who presented these ideas to see what they were like, tested new skills, and tried out living with others in a close relationship—others who were doing these same things. This is what the folk highschool is about. It is what all real education is about. I believe that it is also what life is about.

Annotated Bibliography

I would like to suggest here a limited number of readings on the subject treated in this book. There are many worthwhile things which aren't included, just as there are many worthwhile people whose names are never mentioned by those who write about educational reform or revolution. Some of the books listed here you may have read; you may have read others which you feel are more important than these. Also, the books listed here have, themselves, bibliographies which can lead you further into the subject of alternatives in education.

You will notice that there are no books here called "Strategies for Curriculum Change" or "New Priorities in the Curriculum," or similar titles. This is not an oversight. I have read a horrendous number of books on education, curriculum, educational change, curriculum change, etc., and my conviction is that it is not in such places we must look in times of educational crises as serious as these. Somehow, changing the curriculum, and laboring to come forth with priorities for a new curriculum, implies that someone, we, the experts, know what is best, what is important, what is of value, what it is students *must* learn. On the basis of my own experience in education, I would say that this is at best a shaky assumption.

I have grouped the books into a number of categories which they seem to fall into fairly naturally.

On the Folk Highschools

Olive Dame Campbell, *The Danish Folk High School.* New York: Macmillan, 1928.

> This is one of the best descriptions of the folk highschools by an American. Mrs. Campbell came back home to found a folk highschool in the South. The school was one of the few successful ones to be started in this country, mainly, I believe, because she used the principles and philosophy of the Danish schools and fitted them to the needs of the southern mountain people the school served.

Noelle Davies, *Education for Life: A Danish Pioneer.* London: Williams & Norgate, 1931.

> An Englishman who was quite involved with the folk highschools—he taught at the International People's College at Elsinore—writes about them.

Joseph K. Hart, *Light from the North: The Danish Folk High Schools, Their Meanings for America.* New York: Henry Holt, 1927.

111

Hart was one of those American educators we hear so little about; one of the ones who, in the twenties, were saying that education had to be more than about subjects, that it had to have relevance to the student's life and goals. He went to Denmark to see for himself what the folk highschools were all about and came away highly enthusiastic and sure that we could benefit from their example.

Thomas Rørdam, *The Danish Folk High Schools.* Copenhagen: Det Danske Selskab, 1965.

The most up-to-date book for an overall picture of the highschools. It gives statistics, history, philosophy, describes the different kinds of folk highschools, even has some pictures. It is well written and very interesting.

The Need for a Change

Edgar Z. Friedenberg, *Coming of Age in America, Growth and Acquiescence.* New York: Random House, 1965.

Friedenberg documents the extent to which young people in school have had their pride destroyed, the extent to which they have internalized society's and the school's uncomplimentary picture of them. In a study conducted at two of the country's "best" high schools, he found that to a degree wholly unexpected by him that the students, even the most rebellious of them, had apparently accepted the school's evaluation of their behavior, so that even when they were rebelling against obviously unreasonable and repressive rules, they saw their own behavior as "sick," as deviant. True, this study was made before the current level of student awareness, but I don't believe conditions have changed very much in most schools.

Paul Goodman, *Compulsory Mis-Education and the Community of Scholars.* New York: Random House, 1966.

Goodman believes that school as we know it, institutionalized education, is at best inefficient and boring, and at worst damaging to the children who are forced to undergo it. He argues that scholars and teachers must disassociate themselves from institutions and form small nuclear schools, communities of scholars, scattered about the countryside and cities.

Jonathan Kozol, *Death at an Early Age.* Boston: Houghton Mifflin Company, 1967.

Perhaps one of the most valuable things about this sobering account of the brutal and humiliating treatment of children in the public schools of that stronghold of American culture, Boston, is the clarity with which it shows the virtual impossibility of fighting the system from within. Kozol found himself unable to help the very kids who needed his help the most; he found himself standing by helplessly as fourth graders were whipped for having offended some other teacher. Kozol did not start out a rebel. He was forced gradually into that position as the realities of the system became clear. He tried to fight the system but he was unable to beat it (has anyone?). The kids remained; Kozol was fired two weeks before the end of the year.

Leo Tolstoy, *Tolstoy on Education*. Tr. by Lee Wiener. Chicago: University of Chicago Press, 1967.

One of the most fascinating things about looking into the past of education is finding that it's all been said before. Way back then (about a century ago) Tolstoy was saying that the only real education begins with a question in the life of the learner. He also noted that there were as many "only true methods" of teaching reading as there were reading experts. The one thing they all had in common: none knew more about teaching reading than any other.

Tolstoy started a "free school" to put into practice his ideas about education, but it proved unsuccessful. The book is a collection of various of his writings, including those concerning the "free school" at Yásnaya Polyána.

Getting Our Thinking Unstuck

Robert Bickner, "After the Future, What?" in *Inventing Education for the Future*. Ed. Werner Z. Hirsch. San Francisco: Chandler Publishing Company, 1967.

This is a very thought-provoking chapter in an interesting book. The title of the book suggests the tone: education in the future may well be completely different from what we call education today. This is so much so, says Bickner, that our traditional methods of predicting the future by projecting the past may just prove insufficient. We should be dealing, he says, more with the *possible* than with the *probable*. The probable is, after all, merely what would happen if nothing changed.

Nathaniel Cantor, *The Teaching⇄Learning Process.* New York: Dryden Press, 1953.

This is another book which has greatly influenced me. Cantor, who was a professor of sociology and criminology, believed, as the title suggests, that education is a two way interactive process. He rejected lecturing as merely a substitute for reading, and felt that the most important thing a teacher could do was to act as catalyst. At the beginning of a semester, he had the habit of entering the classroom, taking one of the chairs and just sitting, waiting for what would happen. When the students became frustrated and demanded that he tell them what the course was about and what they were to do, he would return the question to them, asking them why they were there, and what they *intended* to do. In discussions he would refuse to be referee or judge, offering his opinion when he felt it was appropriate, encouraging shy students to participate, continually returning the responsibility for learning to the students.

To be sure, his methods require a strong will (it is so easy to fall into the role of mentor, of wise man), and frustrated many of his students immensely. But the majority blossomed under the experience and declared that it made them reexamine their ideas of what education was about and who it was for. Certainly every teacher should confront the ideas in this book.

Jerry Farber, *The Student as Nigger*. New York: Ballentine Books, 1970.

This is really a book to get our thinking unstuck. The title article gives us a good jolt. If you don't find yourself in his description of the student tugging his forelock in the presence of his teachers, and shuffling his feet in deference, then you had a different kind of education than I did. Other chapters include a hilarious and devastating treatment of how to teach walking—the way we teach reading.

S. I. Hayakawa, *Language in Thought and Action*. New York: Harcourt, Brace and Company, 1949.

Though he, himself, has decisively left the movement, Hayakawa's book remains perhaps the best introduction to general semantics—the study of how language affects the user, how "words use men," how language often *prevents* communication instead of aiding it. (Note the difference between semantics, a branch of philosophy, which tries to pin down exact meanings, and general semantics, which is more a study of the *effects* of words on men.)

If you have not investigated general semantics by all means do. You may be interested to discover that you, too, mistake the map for the territory, that you use "magic" words, that you had forgotten that Bessie [1] is not Bessie [2] is not Bessie.[3] Your tour, under Professor Hayakawa, will be enjoyable and intriguing.

John Holt, *How Children Fail*. New York: Pitman Publishing Company, 1964.

A shocking book, not because it portrays brutality, as does Jonathan Kozol's *Death at an Early Age*, but because it shows those of us who have believed that we were on the side of the children and were attuned to their wavelength the extent to which we were deceived. Even as I was excited by what Holt says, I cringed as he described the ways in which we are cut off from what is really happening to the children in the classroom, things which applied to me, too. John Trivett, one of the best and most inventive teachers today, used to tell us, "Listen to the kids." Holt's book shows us just how far we are from following that advice.

Neil Postman and Charles Weingartner, *Teaching as a Subversive Activity*. New York: Delacorte Press, 1969.

Postman and Weingartner, who are college teachers, have prepared for us a check sheet, so to speak, for the teacher who wants to deal with things that are meaningful to students, in a way which is meaningful. They believe that a teacher, like Hemingway's writer, must have a "built-in crap detector." Much of this book serves to remind us of all the crap which does go on in the classroom, even in spite of us. The authors also declare that one of the primary purposes of an education must be to equip the students with their own crap detectors (this is the subversive activity mentioned in the title—it is obviously subversive to teach students to question formerly unquestioned assumptions). Obviously this is not what schools do now. Besides all its other useful and entertaining offerings, the book has an excellent bibliography.

Alan W. Watts, *The Book On the Taboo Against Knowing Who You Are*. New York: The Macmillan Company, 1967.

In his calm, humorous way, Alan Watts presents us with the most fantastic ideas: how we're deceived by our ideas of cause and effect; how there is neither order nor chaos in nature—that both ideas are human inventions, nature just *is* (at least that's how I understood it); how the most strongly enforced of all taboos in society is the one against finding out who or what you really are, behind the mask of your apparently separate, independent and isolated ego.

Maybe he's saying: take another look, it may all be a fake, or it may not be there at all. Before you commit yourself to society's world be sure it's there, and that you want it. What he says has a great deal to do with self-awareness. We think of the ego, he says, "as if there sat beneath the dome of the skull a controlling officer who wears earphones wired to the ears, and watches a television screen wired to the eyes . . . (he thus controls all our actions). All this can get marvelously complicated when we begin to wonder whether our officer has another officer inside *his* head, and so *ad infinitum!*"

Watts is a great aid in breaking away. He helps to explain in clear, simple-to-understand terms, what we may have suspected all along, or what we saw in a flash of inspiration but were unable to explain, or even what we had never dreamed of.

What Is a School? Some possibilities

George Dennison, *The Lives of Children*. New York: Random House, 1969.

"José's reading problem is José. Or to put it another way, there is no such thing as a reading problem. Jose hates books, schools, and teachers, and among a hundred other insufficiencies—all of a piece—he cannot read. Is this a reading problem?

"A reading problem, in short, is not a fact of life, but a fact of school administration. It does not describe José, but describes the action performed by the school; i.e., the action of ignoring everything about José except his response to printed letters." (from the book)

John Holt has said of this book: "for anyone concerned with education . . . I have said that while there were many recently published books on education (my own among them) that I thought they should read, if they felt they had time for only one it should be *The Lives of Children*. It is by far the most perceptive, moving and important book on education that I have ever read, or indeed, ever expect to read." The book describes the lives of twenty-three children, black, white and Puerto Rican, in the small private school in New York where Dennison taught.

John Dewey. Though I really can't recommend a specific work by the fabled philosopher of education, I can recommend that you try him out. One of the strange things about John Dewey is that though most of us have heard of him, and heard how good/bad he was, very few of us have read what he had to say. I discovered this for myself not too many years ago. Though much of what he says may be slow reading, it certainly has a contemporary message. Read him. Discover for yourself that the map is not the territory! (What folks say he said may not always *be* what he said.)

Joseph Featherstone, *The Primary School Revolution in Britain*. (A Pitman/ New Republic reprint). New York: Pitman Publishing Corporation, 1967. (Originally published as three articles in *The New Republic:* "Schools for Children," August 10, 1967; "How Children Learn," September 2, 1967; "Teaching Children to Think," September 9, 1967.)

I think it is healthy to find out that we are not the only enlightened nation on the planet, with the rest of the world consisting of variously benighted savages—an impression which seems to be held by most Americans. Even in the realm of education we seem to think of ourselves as having invented the whole idea. It must come as something of a shock to discover that in England elementary schools are doing something about findings about how children learn, findings about which we are still only talking.

Arithmetic in English infant schools (our elementary schools) is based on activities, is individualized, does not come out of standardized textbooks. The Nuffield plan, which is the scheme around which the arithmetic programs are developed, was worked out by teachers themselves (not by specialists in a university, working on a grant). One consequence is that it had to work, had to be usable. Most American teachers are incredulous when they learn that during arithmetic period English children move around measuring things, weighing things, timing things, pouring water from one thing into another, and in general doing everything but sitting in nice rows working problems. It is impossible to believe that it would work—or that the teachers could stand it. However, it does and they do; at least they seem to.

Caleb Gattegno, *What We Owe Children*. New York: Outerbridge and Dienstfrey, 1970.

It was Caleb Gattegno who, seeing a demonstration of the Cuisenaire rods by their inventor, a Belgian teacher of the blind, saw their potential for teaching, not merely music and simple arithmetic, but more advanced mathematics. It was also Gattegno who developed the unique Words in Color method of teaching reading, a method which uses color to emphasize the regular aspects of spelling to enable nonreaders to decode written language.

In this book Dr. Gattegno states his thesis that in our typical educational situation we are endeavoring to rely on the least efficient function of the human brain, the memory. As much as ninety percent of school work is memorizing. Memory, a computer's strong point, is one of the brain's weak points. It is much more efficient at comparing, at making judgments, at devising new configurations and combinations. Dr. Gattegno suggests that we spend less time on memorizing in school and more on the really human processes—judgment, evaluation, creation, and the essential job of learning to live together.

Susan Gregory, *Hey White Girl*. New York: W. W. Norton & Company, Inc., 1970.

The author, a teen-ager, moved with her Christian activist family to Chicago, where they lived in a Christian community in the black ghetto. She enrolled in an all-black high school. The book is based on a diary she kept during that year. She gradually became accepted by her classmates and made many close friends. She discovered that the black students were much more spontaneous than the white ones she had known in her previous upper middle class neighborhood, much closer to their feelings, and more honest about their emotions. She was impressed by the leadership qualities of many of her new friends.

She makes a very strong case for the importance of the human part of school, human contacts, and comments on her discovery of the relative irrelevance of grades and standardized tests, when compared with warm, human relations. Many of us feel we have some understanding of the reasons the blacks refuse to continue to accept the roles and conditions society has forced on them; many of us also believe we have at least a faint idea of what it must be like to be black in America. Most of us, however, will not have the chance to live on as intimate terms with young black people as Susan Gregory. Through her book we can begin to understand some of these things in a more real way.

James Herndon, *The Way It Spozed to Be*. New York: Bantam Books, 1968. James Herndon taught in a black junior high school. When he found that the students didn't take to the traditional schooling (the way it spozed to be) he decided to try to work with the things they were interested in. He started using class time for top forty hits, the writing and exchanging of "slam books," the chewing of gum, and other things which were anathema in other classrooms. Among the results were many exciting and/or uproarious class sessions (among other less happy ones, of course), an increased amount of interest and learning from the students, a chance for Herndon to really get to know them, and a reluctance on the part of the administration to re-hire him for the next year. Because his enjoyment of the kids comes through in his writing, the book is a chance for us to enjoy them with him.

John Holt, *How Children Learn.* New York: Pitman Publishing Corporation, 1967.

This sequel to *How Children Fail* describes Holt's experiences "just fooling around" with young children, seeing how they learn, what they learn, how their learning can be aided.

Herbert Kohl, *36 Children.* New York: New American Library, 1967.

The 36 children are Kohl's sixth grade class in a Harlem school. The book is a description of the odyssey Kohl and the children took. In order to provide a meaningful educational experience for the children, he found that he had to venture farther and farther afield from the official course of study and the traditional ways of discipline. Kohl became involved in his students' lives and they in his. He took them on field trips and invited them to his apartment. Just when things were beginning to come together, the school year ended. Kohl tells his growing frustration as he kept track of his former students who were once more being ground down by the system, and wondering whether he had actually done them a disservice by allowing them to be human, so that they began to drop their defenses and were rendered all the more vulnerable when exposed again to the inhumanities of the system.

Much of the book is given to the work of the children themselves. It is another book which gives us a glimpse of what can be done, but at the same time shows the forces actively at work preventing it from being done.

Howard Lane, *On Educating Human Beings.* Chicago: Follett Publishing Company, 1964.

Though not well known, Howard Lane was one of the great humane philosophers in education. His field was ostensibly educational psychology, but his interest in students as people extended far beyond the usual limits of psychology. His description of a school for children still is one of the most inviting I have read, and evokes for me a picture of a place where I could wholeheartedly find myself at home. This book is a collection of his writings published by his friends after his death in 1962.

George Leonard, *Education and Ecstacy*. New York: Delacorte Press, 1968.

Leonard, at one point in this book, describes the Fillmore auditorium during a performance by the Jefferson Airplane or The Grateful Dead, as the greatest multi-media learning experience he has found. The lights, the music, the complete participation by those present—this is lacking in our ordinary educational situations. He asks whether official educational experiences couldn't somehow be made more all-involving. He believes they can and part of the book deals with what might be done with the technology we now have available to build a real multi-media school.

The ecstacy referred to is a recognition that our best learning takes place in situations which involve the mind, the body and the spirit—ecstatic situations—and that if we really want to learn that is the kind of situation we must begin to provide.

Hughes Mearns, *Creative Power: The Education of Youth in the Creative Arts*. New York: Dover Publications, Inc., 1958. (originally published in 1929 by Doubleday Doran & Company).

I discovered this book at a crucial time in my teaching career. I had been teaching in an elementary school in northern California for several years when one day, immediately before school was to begin in the fall, I was called to the principal's office where he and the district superintendent together informed me that "you have some very creative ideas and seem to have good rapport with the students, but..." The "but" was that I was to stop being so creative and having such good rapport with the students and begin to toe the line, settle down, do things the way they're "spozed" to be. Naturally I had had discussions of a similar sort in the past, but the suddenness of this attack so shocked and depressed me that I just got into my bus and started driving. Fortunately I ended up in Mendocino, not in a bar but in a well-stocked bookstore, where I found this book. I bought it, took it out to the bus and started reading. I read about half of it before starting home. As I read I began to feel better, and decided not to hand in my resignation, effective immediately, after all. What I discovered from the book was that other teachers really thought as I did and that, in fact, more than forty years ago had experimented with the same ideas I was experimenting with (and being told to stop): freedom for students, self-discipline, elimination of grades as much as possible, lessons arising out of the student' own interests.

Unfortunately, there are still extremely few schools which are as "modern," as far out of the middle ages, as the school Mearns describes from the nineteen-twenties.

A. S. Neill, *Summerhill*. New York: Hart Publishing Company, Inc., 1960.

Neill, a pioneer in the freedom in education movement, describes in this book a school which is really free. Many of us, including myself, would not be able to accept, or even tolerate, the discomfort and inconvenience which he is able to, and which is a result of the great freedom which his students have. However, his experiences show us that it can be done, and that the results, in terms of the lives of human beings, are worth it. It incidentally adds weight to Goodman's contention that all the stuff which we now cram into kids for twelve years, could really be done in three or four if we were working with the kids rather than against them.

Carl Rogers, *Freedom to Learn*. Columbus, Ohio: Charles E. Merrill, 1969.

In this book Rogers sums up his experience as a teacher and an educational innovator. In his classroom he is as student-centered as he is client-centered in his counseling. Students are given the opportunity to be responsible for what they do and how they do it. They grade themselves, on the basis of their own expectations and accomplishments. As a consequence, of course (I say of course because anyone who has experimented with freedom in the classroom has seen similar results), many of the students learned more, in a meaningful way—that is, they not only learned things, but the things they learned made a difference in their lives—while some complained about the lack of direction. Rogers also includes descriptions of others' experiments with freedom in the classroom.

Finally, he presents his plan for educational reform, which makes use of sensitivity training for teachers and administrators. Only teachers and administrators who are able to be honest, to live with change, who are open to their experience, will be able to allow students freedom and will be able to accept the students' needs as valid. The only freedom to learn, Rogers points out, exists in a situation where the teacher is a facilitator of learning, rather than a judge and dispenser of knowledge.

This book has been long awaited by the many teachers who have tried to apply Rogers' client-centered philosophy in their classrooms. It is good to have him turn his attention to a subject which has long been in need of it.

What Is the New Man?

Hubert Bonner, *On Being Mindful of Man*. Boston: Houghton Mifflin, 1965.

This is a beautifully written, at times poetic statement of belief in man. Man, Bonner says, is purposive, moving toward goals which he sets for himself. He seeks freedom because it is the way to self-validation or authenticity. The search for authenticity is the search for one's identity as a person. It is this search which motivates him. Perhaps this means that the meaning of life is to live. Bonner says that "although the fear of death may cause serious emotional disturbances, it is the fear of life, really, that is the source of most of our psychological ills."

Martin Buber, *Between Man and Man*. London: Routledge and Kegan Paul, 1947.

Buber, in this poetically written book, talks about the importance of being on open, intimate, personal terms with the world—an I-Thou relationship instead of an I-It. We have to have an I-It relationship before we can exploit others or nature. It is interesting to consider the similarity between Buber's I-Thou concept, the Zen which Alan Watts introduces us to, and Rogers' concept of psychological health. When Rogers says, for example, that "I am my feelings," it could be said that he is also expressing an I-Thou relationship with his feelings which, in turn, are in a natural I-Thou relationship with the environment. When we trust our feelings, we are, in effect, believing the messages they bring us about our environment, and about ourselves.

Arthur W. Combs, *The Professional Education of Teachers*. Boston: Allyn and Bacon, 1965.

Despite its uncompromising title, this book actually has to do more with humanism than with professional education. What Combs discovered, in the course of a several-year-long project to determine the curriculum which would best provide teachers who were competent in their skill area, innovative, creative, concerned for the students and humane, was that, surprisingly, there was no such curriculum. Those who became the best teachers (with the above qualifications) were those who were creative, innovative, humane people, concerned for the kids. In other words, the best people became the best teachers. (N.F.S. Grundtvig: "First the man, then the teacher.") Tricks and techniques didn't make the difference between good and bad teachers. The only way to provide better teachers is to somehow help people to become better people. Combs comes to the conclusion that, since learning is a human process, "it is the behavior of teachers in classrooms that will finally determine whether or not our schools meet or fail to meet the challenge of our times." To this I would just like to add that the real challenge of our times has nothing to do with beating the communists, is not concerned with the "excellence" of our educational product as measured on a nationwide test, has little or nothing to do with whether our spacemen reach the moon first, but has everything to do with whether man will really finally make the earth uninhabitable for himself, both physically and spiritually (or morally, or psychologically). And it has much to do with whether our schools can become relevant to the needs of the people, become humane in their relationships with them (and with the teachers), become no longer dumping grounds for hundreds of thousands of people we have to keep off the labor market, as they are now, but instead become what they were supposed to have been all along, places where people can become skilled in the arts of living and living together.

Sidney M. Jourard, *The Transparent Self*. New York: D. Van Nostrand, 1964.

Among other things, Jourard has a thought-provoking section on the fact that this human organism has built-in abilities to cure itself of physical diseases (all doctors know this, of course) and he declares that the same is also true of psychological and intellectual diseases. To a great extent the medicines and treatments prescribed by doctors are mainly intended to give the body a chance to get itself cured. By the same token, given a healthy, unthreatening environment, the human psyche can undertake to keep itself in a state of health.

One of the things I like about Jourard is his statement that despite what he had previously written on love—describing it in psychological terms for those to whom this kind of thing is important—one of the most important things about love was that it was pleasureful. This seems to me to have been the case all along, but it's nice to have a psychologist come along.

Carl R. Rogers, *On Becoming a Person*. Boston: Houghton Mifflin Company, 1961.

This is not the "definitive" Rogers, perhaps, but certainly the most inclusive. Certainly if you haven't read this book, or at least browsed through it, you have missed a powerful statement concerning man's real nature, his capacity for positive growth, and a personal statement by one of the great figures in psychology.

Other

I have not listed any of the numerous excellent articles to be found in periodicals, concerning the subjects we have dealt with. To have done so would have extended this bibliography unduly. There are, however, several periodicals, themselves, which demand mention because of their uniqueness. They are:

This Magazine Is about Schools, 56 Esplanade St., East, Suite 301, Toronto 215, Ontaria, Canada. (available by subscription or from better bookstores—by better I mean aware)

Published in Canada, *This Magazine* is what no other educational periodical is: it is radical, concerned with the welfare of children, outspoken, exciting, humorous, provoking, experimental. If you think that everything exciting in education is going on in the States, think again!

The Saturday Review: Education Supplement.

The education supplement, while often dull, is as often a real source of exciting ideas about education.

The Whole Earth Catalog.

Published by the Portola Institute, 558 Santa Cruz Avenue, Menlo Park, California, the *Whole Earth Catalog* represents, for many people, what learning, education, a curriculum, is all about. Contents of the catalogue range from art books to flour mills to books on how to repair your car, to where to get the best loom, potter's wheel, camping equipment, to books on how to build your own geodesic dome, to seed catalogues, to how to find out how to build your own adobe house to. . . .

The function of the *Whole Earth Catalog* is *access to tools.* Tools means books and pamphlets—many available from the government— besides the things we ordinarily think of as "tools," since a tool can be defined as anything which helps us to do a job, whether that job is becoming educated, or informed, building a house, climbing a mountain or weaving a blanket.

If I were starting a school, and needed a catalogue of courses and curriculum guide, I can think of nothing more appropriate, or with more built-in motivation, than the *Whole Earth Catalog.*

PRONUNCIATION GUIDE
TO KEY DANISH WORDS

I have often wished, when reading a book containing foreign terms, that the author had provided some sort of key to help me figure out how the words sounded. I have tried here to select those Danish words and names which are most apt to be mispronounced by the reader unfamiliar with Danish, and to give an approximation of their pronunciation. The approximations are close enough to give the flavor of the original without, however, being exhaustively correct. The simplified key is based on Websters New World Dictionary, College Edition (The World Publishing Company, 1953).

Danish words and names in the text which do not appear here are pronounced enough like they look to present no problems to the reader.

a   fat, lap
ā   ape, date
â   bare, care
ä   car, father
e   ten, let
ē   even, meet
ê   here, dear
ẽ   over, chauffer
i   hit, fit
ī   bite, mile
o   lot, top
ō   go, tone
ô   horn, fork
ö   Fr. *feu*, Ger. *Goethe*
o͞o   tool, troop
oi   oil, boy
ou   out, doubt
u   up, fun
ũr   fur, turn (pronounced as eastern or southern speakers do,
     without the r-coloration, that is, dropping the r's)
ə   a in ago, e in agent
sh   she, dash
th th as in then, father
kh   Ger. *doch*, Scot. *loch*
'   An apostrophe after a consonant indicates that the consonant
     is voiceless and often tends to be left out entirely.
r'   The closest we can come to the Danish r is the French r. The
     vocalized American r, as in *range*, is never used in Danish.
     The Danish r is neither trilled, as in Spanish, nor growled, as
     in German. It is almost not there.
/   The slash indicates that the preceding syllable is accented.

❈   ❈   ❈

Aarhus (ôr'/ho͞os)   the second largest city in Denmark
Askov (as/kōv')
Bukdahl, Jørgen (yör'n bo͞ok/däl)
Copenhagen (kō/pen hä/gen) in Danish: Købnhavn (kö/ben houn/)
Det Danske Selskab (de dan/skə sel/skab)   The Danish Company
Dragsdahl, Johannes (yō han/es dr'ag's/däl)
Fejltokning af Ryslingestriden (fīl/tōlk ning a rēs/ling str'ē *th*en)
folkehøjskoler (folk/ə hoi/skōl ẽr)
folkelig (folk/ə lē)

Grundtvig, Nicolai Frederik Severin (nic/ō lī fr'eth/er' ik sev/er' in grōōnt/vig')
Göteborg (yö/tə bôr'kh)
Hesbjerg (hes/byârg')
Højskolebladet (hoi/sko lə bla/thet) the Folk Highschool Journal
Indre Mission (in/r'ə mi shōn/)
Kierkegaard, Søren (sör'/en kêr'/kə gôr'd)
Koch, Bodil (bō dēl/ kokh)
Kungälv (kōōng/elv)
Magleaas (mou/lê ōs)
Manniche, Peter (pêder' man/nikh ə)
Schrøder, Ludwig (lōōd/vcg shr'ö/der')
Skole (skō/lɔ)
Sorø (sôr'/ö)
Sørensen, Rasmus (sör'/ən sen)
Politiken (pō li tēk/en) a leading Copenhagen newspaper
Rantzauminde (ran/sous min/ne)
Roskilde (r'os/kē lə)
Ryslinge (r'üs/ling ə)
Rødding (r'öd/ing)
Rørdam, Thomas (r'ör'/dam)
Uldum (ōōl/dəm)
Verden (vär/den) the world
Wegener, Johann (yō/han vā/gen er')
Zeeland (in Danish: Sjaelland—shā/land')

INDEX